VEGAN

—— 70 Comforting Plant-Based Recipes ——

JAPAN

Julia Boucachard

THE EXPERIMENT

NEW YORK

VEGAN JAPAN: *70 Comforting Plant-Based Recipes*
Copyright © 2023 by Éditions Solar
Translation copyright © 2024 by The Experiment, LLC

Originally published in French as *Japon Vegan* by Éditions Solar, an imprint of Édi8, Paris, France, in 2023. First published in English in North America by The Experiment, LLC, in 2024.

The Experiment, LLC
220 East 23rd Street, Suite 600
New York, NY 10010-4658
theexperimentpublishing.com

THE EXPERIMENT and its colophon are registered trademarks of The Experiment, LLC. Many of the designations used by manufacturers and sellers to distinguish their products are claimed as trademarks. Where those designations appear in this book and The Experiment was aware of a trademark claim, the designations have been capitalized.

The Experiment's books are available at special discounts when purchased in bulk for premiums and sales promotions as well as for fund-raising or educational use. For details, contact us at info@theexperimentpublishing.com.

Library of Congress Cataloging-in-Publication Data available upon request

ISBN 979-8-89303-006-8
Ebook ISBN 979-8-89303-007-5

Cover and text design by Beth Bugler
Photographs and styling by Manon Gouhier
Illustrations by Sanae Nicolas
Translation by Maggie Kimmich Smith

Manufactured in China

First printing October 2024
10 9 8 7 6 5 4 3 2 1

CONTENTS

Introduction

Although I spent more of my childhood in the French countryside than in Tokyo, I grew up immersed in my mother's Japanese culture. Originally from Osaka, the food capital of Japan, she shared her love of Japanese home cooking with me. The meals she cooked always included a bowl of rice, a side of vegetables, a serving of fish or meat, and a small soup. Coming home from school was always my favorite moment of the day, because I got to treat myself to the delicious dishes my mother had prepared.

I moved between France and Tokyo throughout my childhood, but it wasn't until the age of eleven that I discovered the other side of Japanese cuisine: Not the traditional and healthy dishes prepared at home, but street food and yōshoku, or Western dishes that have been reinvented to suit Japanese tastes.

In Japan, food is displayed everywhere, all the time. Just stroll down the street and you'll pass restaurant windows displaying sampuru, silicone food models that look so realistic they'll make your mouth water. If you keep going, you will eventually come across a yatai, one of the small sidewalk food carts at which people gather to eat savory, stuffed dumplings called *takoyaki*, or *oden*, a classic Japanese stew.

Then, a few steps farther, you will stumble upon a konbini, a sort of 24-7 supermarket, and you will discover all kinds of ready-made snacks: onigiri (stuffed rice balls), instant ramen cups, bento boxes, and even nikuman (steamed, stuffed buns that are sold hot, directly out of a heated display case). Not only that, but there is always a jidōhanbaiki nearby, a vending machine that sells hot and cold drinks, ice cream, and even sometimes fries and grilled onigiri!

If you take the metro, you'll find that certain stations are home to a wide variety of restaurants. Even shopping centers have entire floors dedicated to restaurants, especially famiresu, family-style restaurant chains that commonly serve yōshoku dishes. Famiresu serve dishes like doria (rice gratin in bechamel sauce), hanbāgu (hamburger steak with a *tonkatsu* demi-glace), and even wafū pasta (literally, "Japanese-style pasta").

My palate was expanded by these new flavors and ways of cooking, but I never lost my love for my mother's homecooked meals. My appreciation for traditional Japanese cooking only grew as I began to discover the huge variety of vegetables available in Japan. The Japanese landscape is blanketed in mountains and forests that cover 70 percent of the country. While this leaves little space for the large fields needed to breed animals, it provides favorable conditions for cultivating an incredible variety of vegetables, roots, tubers, and herbs that aren't found in Europe. Japanese vegetables are generally smaller and have a softer skin and sweeter flesh than those in the West, and the Japanese embrace seasonal cooking to take advantage of their flavor.

Some varieties of vegetables are named for the region where they were first produced nearly a thousand years ago, like the shōgoin daikon, a white turnip from Shōgoin (eastern Kyoto), or the kamonasu, an eggplant from Kamo (northern Kyoto). It is no coincidence that Kyoto produces such a large variety of fruits and vegetables: The city is located far from the ocean and has always had difficulty sourcing fresh fish, so vegetables quickly took a central place in inhabitants' diets. Kyoto is also the birthplace of shōjin ryōri, the completely vegan cuisine of the Buddhist monks whose religion forbade killing animals for human consumption.

The seasons in Japan are more distinct than in France and allow plants to fully develop through their different cycles. The Japanese calendar includes seventy-two micro-seasons, each marking a transformation in nature. Each transition from one season to another is celebrated by a feast or a matsuri, a traditional festival. For example, Setsubun is celebrated on February 3 and marks the transition to spring, and Tsukimi welcomes autumn and pays tribute to the moon. The seasons play an incredibly important role in Japanese peoples' lives but also in their diet. The people are vigilant when it comes to eating seasonally, to benefit as much as possible from the nutrient-dense fruit and vegetables, but also because seasonal produce simply tastes better.

My mother passed these values on to me. My meals have always been veggie-heavy, so I never understood why my classmates disliked spinach or mushrooms so much. They usually preferred a plate of fries with a slice of ham. For my part, I didn't care much for meat because I wasn't particularly fond of the taste or texture. However, I did like the sauce that came with it. So, after I learned about the brutal reality of slaughterhouse practices, going vegetarian was a natural choice for me. After that, it just seemed logical to become vegan.

But I had trouble finding vegan options in restaurants, especially in Japanese restaurants, where nearly all the dishes contain meat or fish. So, I began to veganize my mother's recipes: kombu dashi (a broth made from kombu seaweed) replaces dashi with katsuobushi (dried bonito), tofu substitutes ground meat, and oyster mushrooms stand in for seafood. It was a walk in the park! It isn't difficult to make a recipe vegan when the cuisine is already so focused on vegetables. The biggest challenges have been replacing the unprocessed raw ingredients, especially eggs, and reproducing textures such as *fuwa fuwa*, the soft, airy texture of Japanese cakes and breads, but even these can be achieved with some creative substitutions.

After more than a year of tests and preparation, I opened my restaurant, Mori Café, in 2020 in the 11th arrondissement of Paris. I wanted to share the authenticity and diversity of Japanese cuisine while also showing the skeptics that vegan cuisine can be gourmet. For this reason, I offer à la carte dishes that change with the seasons, such as a Japanese kabocha squash curry, a winter vegetable stew, or a chilled noodle dish in the summer.

My experience running Mori Café is what inspired me to create this book of recipes for you. After exploring every nook and cranny of vegan Japanese cuisine, I felt it was important to share its secrets so that as many people as possible realize that today we can eat well while also adhering to a diet that is respectful and considerate of animals and nature.

I begin the book with a description of the basic Japanese ingredients you'll need, and recipes for essential sauces and condiments. All the recipes are classified by both category (main dishes, side dishes, street foods, and desserts) and season, so you can make use of this book while respecting the cycles of nature.

Essential Ingredients

Soy and rice are two staples in Japanese cuisine. Rice is used to make sake, mirin, and rice vinegar, and soy is the base of soy sauce, miso, and tofu. All of these ingredients will certainly be found in every Japanese kitchen, as they are the foundation of countless Japanese dishes! These products can be stored for a long time in the refrigerator.

Rice

Rice for the Japanese is like bread for the French. It is a starch that almost always accompanies our meals. Make sure to choose a Japanese rice, which has round, short, translucent grains that become slightly sticky once cooked. High-quality Japanese rice is delicious, even without seasoning. If you normally add sauce to your rice bowls, I invite you to try it plain to appreciate its natural taste! There are many varieties in Japan, but a smaller selection is available abroad. I recommend *koshihikari* rice, which is fairly easy to find at Asian markets. The Yumenishiki brand is a fairly good value for your money.

HOW TO COOK RICE

Most Japanese people use a rice cooker, but if you don't have one at home, you can use a pot. Each step in its preparation is important for perfect rice.

To make 4 to 5 servings:

- Weigh 2 cups (400 g) rice in a large bowl and cover it completely with water. Gently rub the grains between your fingers, then strain the cloudy water. Repeat this action two or three times, until the water runs clear.

- Strain the rice and let stand for 15 minutes to dry.

- Pour the rice into a medium pot and add 2 cups (480 ml) water (preferably filtered or mineral water). Cover the pot and bring to a boil. Reduce the heat and cook over low for 12 to 15 minutes. Turn off the heat and let the rice stand, covered, for 15 minutes. (Never remove the lid during the cooking process.)

- Once the rice is cooked, fluff it with a fork or a dampened shamoji (rice paddle).

Mirin

Mirin is a type of rice wine, not to be confused with sake. It contains less alcohol than sake and has a thicker texture and sweeter taste. There are several types, but hon mirin is a good option that is easy to find.

To make a quick mirin substitute at home, add ¼ cup (50 g) sugar and ¼ cup plus 3 tablespoons (100 ml) sake to a saucepan over low heat and stir until the sugar is dissolved. Store in an airtight jar in the refrigerator for up to 1 month.

Sake

Sake is an alcohol made by fermenting rice with kōji mold, the same product used to make soy sauce and miso. An inexpensive sake is fine for cooking.

Rice Vinegar

Aside from its many health benefits, rice vinegar is added to rice to make it easier to handle when making sushi or onigiri.

Soy Sauce

Also known as shōyu, there are now many brands of soy sauce available abroad, but I recommend opting for Japanese brands, which I believe have a more authentic taste.

You will most often find shōyu koikuchi (dark soy sauce), the soy sauce most commonly used in Japanese cooking, but shōyu usukuchi (light soy sauce) is used occasionally. Shōyu usukuchi can be found at Asian markets; it is better suited than koikuchi for use in sauces, due to its lighter color and saltier flavor profile. Tamari should not be used as a one-to-one substitute, as it has a more pronounced flavor than soy sauce.

Miso

Miso paste is an absolute gem in Japanese cooking. It is an umami concentrate that will add intense savory flavor to your dishes.

In the same way rice is fermented to make sake, soybeans are fermented with kōji, which is inoculated with a type of grain. There are many types of miso, of which there are two most common: red (aka) and white (shiro) miso. For main dishes and miso soup, I recommend using red miso because it is more full-bodied. White miso is milder and goes well with vegetables and light dishes.

Note that some miso varieties sold in Asian markets contain fish dashi. Check the ingredients or avoid those labeled だし入り ("contains dashi").

Tofu

I find tofu to be underappreciated abroad. People don't often consider eating it as is, with a little soy sauce or wasabi, as we do in Japan. Just like white rice, a high-quality tofu is delicious plain.

Tofu comes in different textures, usually silken (soft) and firm. In vegan cooking, silken tofu is often used in sweet recipes, and firm tofu is often an alternative to meat in savory recipes. I like to use smoked firm tofu as a meat alternative because the flavor adds savory depth.

Vegan Dashi

Many Japanese recipes for dashi, or broth, contain katsuobushi (dried bonito flakes). Bonito is a kind of fish, and it's used as an ingredient in many sauces and dishes for its robust umami flavor. In vegan cuisine, we replace the fish with kombu seaweed and shiitake mushrooms. These two ingredients are packed with a ton of umami flavor and will serve as a good base for your dashi.

You can make your own dashi from scratch, or you can use kombu dashi powder or shiitake dashi, which can be found in large supermarket chains.

Kombu Dashi Powder

Made from dried seaweed, this powder is a light and aromatic bouillon with a flavor close to that of traditional bonito dashi. You can make your own kombu dashi (see page 14) or use a store-bought powder. The latter is particularly useful when you want to make a milk-based rather than a water-based broth, like for Tantanmen (page 41), and concentrated sauces such as Ponzu Sauce (page 17).

Shiitake Mushrooms

These large mushrooms have a strong aroma and are sold fresh or dried at Asian markets. They are used widely in Japanese cuisine to add chewiness to dishes as well as umami depth.

Shimeji Mushrooms

These small white mushrooms are easily recognizable by their elongated stems. They are sold in clusters and have a slightly nutty taste when cooked. They're almost always eaten cooked, as they have a bitter taste when raw. Both the stem and cap are edible.

Enoki Mushrooms

These delicate white mushrooms grow in bundles and are very nutritious and flavorful. They cook quickly and are added to many Japanese dishes, including ramen.

Toasted Sesame Oil

This fragrant oil is widely used in Japanese and other Asian cuisines. It has a rather low smoke point, so I usually recommend waiting to add it to your dishes at the end of cooking or using it to season cold dishes.

Rayu Chile Oil

Rayu is a sesame oil infused with spices and peppers. It is very popular in Japanese cuisine and adds a fiery bite to dishes. It is often available on the table in restaurants.

Fresh Garlic and Ginger

Widely used in Japanese cookery (and in Asian cuisine in general), garlic and ginger are indispensable seasonings to have in your kitchen. Their flavors give dishes a lift and meld beautifully with soy sauce and miso.

They taste different depending on whether they are minced, julienned, or finely chopped, which is why different recipes call for different preparation methods.

Potato Starch

Potato starch (*katakuriko* in Japanese) is particularly useful in vegan cookery to thicken sauces and liquids. It is also used as a coating or mixed with flour for frying. If you can't find potato starch, cornstarch is an acceptable alternative.

Kala Namak

Kala namak, or Himalayan black salt, comes from salt mines in the Himalayas. It is kiln-fired with sulfur-rich harad seeds, giving it a distinctive "eggy" taste. Very strong in flavor, it should be used sparingly.

Tonkatsu Sauce

Tonkatsu sauce is a thick brown sauce that is traditionally served with breaded dishes. It is simultaneously sour, sweet, and spicy, its flavor somewhat reminiscent of barbecue sauce. It can be made at home, but vegan varieties are available if you prefer to purchase a premade version, notably the popular brand Otafuku.

Aburaage (Fried Tofu)

Aburaage is thinly sliced twice-fried tofu. You can buy it premade in the refrigerator aisle of Asian markets. I use it in several recipes in this book, such as Nabe (page 38), Oinari-San (page 48) and Kitsune Udon (page 73).

Daikon

The white radish, or daikon, is a root vegetable that is widely used in Japan. It is juicy and slightly spicy and is commonly eaten raw or pickled. Daikon is easily found in Asian markets and some supermarkets. Make sure to choose a firm one to ensure that it is crunchy.

Kabocha Squash

Kabocha squash is native to Japan. It is squat and round with rough green skin and pale-yellow flesh. If you can't find it, buttercup squash or another winter squash is an acceptable substitute.

Shichimi Togarashi

This mix of spices and pepper elevates cooked dishes and is often available on the table in Japanese restaurants. It is made from powdered red pepper as well as sesame seeds or even seaweed, depending on the recipe. It brings umami to dishes and is a perfect complement to ramen as well as tofu or grilled vegetables.

Nori, Wakame, and Kombu Seaweed

Nori seaweed is very rich in protein. It is sold in sheets that can be cut to make maki or onigiri or used to garnish a bowl of ramen. It is also available in a powdered form that can be used to sprinkle over dishes. Wakame seaweed can be eaten in salads or soups and is sold fresh or dried. *Kombu* is a generic term that designates diverse types of edible seaweed. Generally sold dried and cut into strips, it is a key element of dashi.

BASICS

Kombu Dashi

Season Year-round
Prep Time 5 minutes
Cook Time 10 minutes
Makes about 3¼ cups (780 ml)

In Japan, dashi, or broth, is primarily made with dried bonito flakes, katsuobushi. Kombu is also used, but kombu dashi is more difficult to find and often contains katsuobushi. Making kombu dashi is very simple, but the seaweed can make the dashi bitter if it is infused for too long, so I recommend removing the kombu from the broth once it starts to become slimy during the cooking.

1. Add the cold water and kombu to a large pot over medium heat. Just before the water comes to a boil, use a slotted spoon to remove the kombu, then let the liquid simmer for 10 minutes. Use the slotted spoon to skim off any foam that forms on top.

2. Turn off the heat. Let the dashi cool and store it in an airtight container in the refrigerator for up to 1 week.

4¼ cups (1 L) cold water

One 5-inch (13 cm) square kombu sheet, torn into 3 or 4 pieces

Shiitake Dashi

Season Year-round
Prep Time 5 minutes
Cook Time 10 minutes
Makes about 3 cups (720 ml)

Another alternative to katsuobushi dashi is shiitake dashi. Shiitake mushrooms have a strong umami flavor and add incredible depth to the dashi.

1. Rinse the mushrooms in a colander until the water runs clear.

2. Add the mushrooms and 4¼ cups (1 L) water to a medium pot over high heat. Bring to a boil, using a slotted spoon to skim any foam that forms on top. Reduce the heat to medium-low and cover the pot. Simmer for about 10 minutes.

3. Strain the broth through a fine-mesh strainer set over a bowl and discard the mushrooms. Let the broth cool before storing it in an airtight container in the refrigerator for up to 1 week.

6 large dried shiitake mushrooms (see Note)

NOTE: Dried shiitakes are sold in Asian markets and in some supermarkets or health food stores.

Mitarashi Sauce

Season *Year–round*
Prep Time *5 minutes*
Cook Time *5 minutes*
Serves *2*

This soy-based sauce is a necessity when enjoying Dango Mochi (page 138). Its syrupy texture pairs perfectly with the soft rice balls and other skewers and kebabs, which add a smoky flavor to the sweet-salty sauce. The sauce doesn't keep well (it solidifies at room temperature and in the refrigerator), so I recommend using it immediately.

Add the cold water, sugar, soy sauce, and potato starch to a small saucepan and stir until the potato starch is dissolved. Cook over medium heat and continue to stir until the sauce begins to thicken, about 4 minutes, then quickly remove it from the heat as the sauce will thicken rapidly! The sauce should be thick but pourable. Serve immediately by pouring over dango mochi.

- **¼ cup (60 ml) cold water**
- **3 tablespoons sugar**
- **1 tablespoon soy sauce**
- **2 teaspoons potato starch or cornstarch**

Ponzu Sauce

Season Year-round
Prep Time 5 minutes
Cook Time 5 minutes
Makes 1½ cups (360 ml)

Ponzu is a popular dipping sauce made from soy and citrus. You can use sudachi, a green Japanese citrus fruit; yuzu, a yellow citrus fruit with notes of grapefruit; or even kabosu, slightly larger than the sudachi and highly acidic. I have a personal preference for yuzu because it gives the sauce a distinct flavor, but you can use whichever you prefer.

1. Add the mirin and rice vinegar to a small saucepan and bring to a boil over high heat.

2. As soon as the mixture begins to boil, turn off the heat and add the soy sauce, dashi powder, and yuzu juice. Stir and let cool.

3. Store the sauce in an airtight container in the refrigerator for up to 4 months.

½ cup (120 ml) mirin

¼ cup plus 3 tablespoons (100 ml) rice vinegar

½ cup plus 1 teaspoon (125 ml) usukuchi soy sauce

1 tablespoon kombu dashi powder

1 teaspoon yuzu juice

Demi-Glace Sauce

Season *Year-round*
Prep Time *5 minutes*
Cook Time *1 hour*
Makes *2 cups (480 ml)*

I first discovered demi-glace at a famiresu (family-style restaurant), and ever since, it has been one of my favorite sauces. A traditional French demi-glace sauce is made from a base of beef stock infused with tomato paste and herbs. In Japan, it is used in many yōshoku, or Western-style Japanese dishes, such as omuraisu and Hayashi rice. The traditional recipe is quite long and tedious to make, so my mother would use tonkatsu sauce, which is a mixture of vegetables, fruit, and aromatics, as a base. Just add red wine and a little soy sauce, and you've got a demi-glace!

1. Add the wine to a small saucepan and bring it to a boil over high heat to cook off the alcohol, about 5 minutes.

2. Add the tonkatsu sauce, tomato sauce, soy sauce, sugar, and bay leaves, and stir. Reduce the heat to medium and let the sauce simmer for about 1 hour, stirring occasionally, until it's thick and smooth.

3. Serve warm, or store in an airtight container in the refrigerator for up to 2 weeks.

- **½ cup plus 2 tablespoons (150 ml) red wine**
- **½ cup plus 2 tablespoons (150 ml) tonkatsu sauce**
- **½ cup plus 2 tablespoons (150 ml) tomato sauce (passata)**
- **¼ cup plus 1 tablespoon (75 ml) usukuchi soy sauce**
- **¼ cup plus 2 tablespoons (75 g) sugar**
- **2 bay leaves**

Miso Glaze

Season Year-round
Prep Time 5 minutes
Cook Time 5 minutes
Makes 1¼ cups (300 ml)

For anyone with a sweet tooth, nothing is better than this miso glaze! It is also a true umami bomb, as miso is rich in glutamate, an amino acid responsible for savory flavor. This sauce is great paired with Eggplant Dengaku (page 95).

1. Add the mirin, sake, and sugar to a saucepan over high heat. Bring to a boil and cook for 2 to 3 minutes to let the alcohol evaporate. (If you want a thicker sauce, continue simmering for another 4 to 5 minutes.)
2. Turn off the heat and add the miso. Whisk the sauce until smooth and there are no small pieces of miso left.
3. Let the sauce cool before storing it in an airtight container in the refrigerator for up to 3 weeks.

¼ cup plus 3 tablespoons (100 ml) mirin

¼ cup plus 3 tablespoons (100 ml) sake

¼ cup plus 2 tablespoons (75 g) sugar

¾ cup (200 g) white miso

Hiyashi Chūka Vinaigrette

Season Summer
Prep Time 5 minutes
Serves 5

Ever since I was a child, summer in Japan has reminded me of salads and cold noodle dishes. There are many different chilled noodle dishes that we enjoy when the sun is shining: zaru udon, thick wheat noodles; sōmen, very thin noodles; zaru soba, cold buckwheat noodles; or hiyashi chūka, a cold yakisoba noodle dish. Unlike other noodle dishes, hiyashi chūka noodles are not eaten by dipping them in a sauce (such as mentsuyu), but rather are topped with a vinaigrette made from soy sauce and sesame oil. Sweet, tart, and fragrant with sesame, it is simultaneously refreshing and rich, perfect for summer.

Combine the sesame oil, rice vinegar, soy sauce, and sugar with ⅔ cup plus 1 tablespoon (175 ml) water in a medium bowl. Whisk until the oil is well emulsified with the rest of the mixture. Store the sauce in an airtight container in the refrigerator for up to 3 weeks.

- ⅔ cup plus 1 tablespoon (175 ml) toasted sesame oil
- ½ cup plus 2 tablespoons (150 ml) rice vinegar
- ⅔ cup plus 1 tablespoon (175 ml) soy sauce
- ¼ cup plus 2 tablespoons (75 g) sugar

Teriyaki Sauce

Season Year-round
Prep Time 5 minutes
Cook Time 20 minutes
Makes about 1¾ cups (420 ml)

Teriyaki sauce is one of the most iconic Japanese sauces. It is made from a base of soy sauce and sugar, and pairs well with meat, salmon, and tofu. When I was young, my mother often prepared a big batch of teriyaki with ground beef and ginger, which I would grab from the refrigerator and dish out onto a steaming bowl of rice when I needed a snack. I still enjoy this sweet and savory treat—just with plant-based ground meat now!

1. Add the mirin, sugar, and sake to a small saucepan and bring to a boil over medium heat. Boil for 10 minutes to cook off the alcohol and thicken the mixture, then reduce the heat to low and stir in the soy sauce. Simmer for 10 minutes.

2. Remove the sauce from the heat and let cool completely.

3. Store in an airtight container in the refrigerator for up to 1 month.

- ½ cup plus 2 tablespoons (150 ml) mirin
- ¼ cup plus 2 tablespoons (75 g) sugar
- 3 tablespoons sake
- ½ cup plus 2 tablespoons (150 ml) usukuchi soy sauce

Mentsuyu

Season *Summer*
Prep Time *10 minutes*
Cook Time *5 minutes*
Makes *1¼ cups (300 ml)*

Mentsuyu is a concentrated sauce made from soy sauce and dashi. It's often served diluted as a dipping sauce for cold noodles.

1 large shiitake mushroom

½ cup plus 2 tablespoons (150 ml) mirin

½ cup plus 1 teaspoon (125 ml) soy sauce

¼ cup (60 ml) sake

One 5-inch (13 cm) square kombu sheet, broken into 3 to 4 pieces

1. Rinse the mushroom under cold running water until the water runs clear, then let dry for a few minutes.

2. Add the mushroom, mirin, soy sauce, sake, and kombu to a small saucepan. Bring to a boil over medium heat, then reduce the heat and simmer for 5 minutes.

3. Turn off the heat and strain the sauce through a fine-mesh strainer set over a bowl, discarding the solids. If any debris remains, strain a second time. The sauce can be stored in an airtight container in the refrigerator for up to 4 months.

4. To serve cold, either dilute 1 part concentrated sauce with 1 to 1½ parts cold water, or combine the desired amount of mentsuyu with an equal volume of ice cubes which will gradually melt during the meal (my preferred method). To serve hot, dilute 1 part mentsuyu with 2 to 3 parts boiling water.

Udon Noodles

Season *Year-round*
Prep Time *1 hour*
Chill Time *6 hours*
Cook Time *10 to 15 minutes*
Serves *3 to 4*

Whether you prefer them hot or cold, everyone loves udon noodles. They are unique among Japanese noodles because they contain gluten, a stretchy protein found in certain grains like wheat. The dough is traditionally kneaded by foot (after first being covered with a clean cloth) to develop the gluten and give the udon its signature texture: soft, with a firm interior. Kneading the dough takes some patience, but the results are worth it!

1. Sift the flour into a large bowl. To a second bowl, add the salt and ¾ cup plus 2 tablespoons (210 ml) water. Stir until the salt has completely dissolved.

2. Pour a quarter of the salted water into the bowl of flour and mix well by hand. The mixture will look dry and crumbly. Add another quarter of the water and mix again. Repeat until there are only a few tablespoons of water remaining in the bottom of the bowl. (The remaining water will be used to moisten the dough as needed.)

3. Working directly in the bowl, form a ball of dough by pressing it with your palm. (Add more water, a bit at a time, if the dough doesn't come together. When there are only a few dry crumbs left behind, stop adding water or the dough could become too sticky.)

4. Place the dough ball in a large ziplock plastic bag but do not seal it. Place a clean kitchen towel on a section of floor. Place the bagged dough on the towel, and then cover it with a second clean towel.

5. Step lightly on the bagged dough in several places to flatten it and spread it to the edges of the bag. Once flat, remove the dough from the bag, fold it into thirds, and then return it to the bag and step on it again until you flatten it once more. Repeat this action 5 to 6 times, then fold the dough into thirds one last time.

4 cups (500 g) cake flour

5 teaspoons salt

Potato starch or cornstarch, for working the dough

6. Seal the dough inside the plastic bag to prevent it from drying, then chill it in the refrigerator for 3 hours.

7. Form the chilled dough into a ball again by rolling the outer edges toward the center. Press lightly to flatten.

8. Place the dough back inside the plastic bag and return to the refrigerator for another 3 hours.

9. Dust your work surface lightly with potato starch, then use a rolling pin to spread the dough to form a square 1 to 2 inches (2.5–5 cm) thick.

10. Sprinkle both sides of the dough lightly with potato starch and fold it into thirds, then dust with more potato starch. For round noodles, use a rolling pin to shape the dough into a rectangle $\frac{1}{8}$- to $\frac{1}{4}$-inch (3–6 mm) thick and use a knife to cut strips of equal width and thickness. For flat noodles, roll the dough into a $\frac{1}{16}$ to $\frac{1}{8}$-inch (2–3 mm) thick rectangle and use a knife to cut strips $\frac{1}{2}$- to $\frac{3}{4}$-inch (1.25–2 cm) wide. Arrange the noodles into several loose piles.

11. Bring a large pot of water to a boil over high heat and gently add the noodles. Reduce the heat and simmer for 10 to 15 minutes, depending on the thickness of your noodles. To test the noodles for doneness, once they begin to look slightly translucent, run a noodle under cold water to stop the cooking, then taste. When it no longer tastes salty, you can drain all the noodles and rinse them 2 to 3 times with cold water to stop their cooking.

12. Serve the cooked noodles immediately.

Japanese Mayonnaise

Season Year–round
Prep Time 5 minutes
Makes about 1½ cups (350 g)

Kewpie is the most popular mayonnaise brand in Japan. Smooth and slightly sweet, it's often incorporated into hot dishes like okonomiyaki, karaage, and yakisoba. It brings indisputable richness and umami to dishes because its manufacturers add MSG, an additive widely used in the Japanese food industry. However, as this recipe shows, you don't need MSG to achieve umami flavor.

1. Add the tofu and lemon juice to a blender and blend until just smooth.

2. Add the sugar, kombu dashi powder, and rice vinegar to a small bowl and stir until the sugar is dissolved, then pour it all into the tofu mixture and blend until well combined.

3. With the blender running, gradually drizzle in the oil to create an emulsion. (If you want a thicker mayonnaise, continue adding more oil until the desired texture is achieved.)

4. Once you finish adding the oil, add the kala namak and blend just until combined.

5. Store the mayonnaise in an airtight container in the refrigerator for up to 1 week.

¾ cup (200 g) silken tofu

1 tablespoon plus 2 teaspoons lemon juice

1 tablespoon sugar

1½ teaspoons kombu dashi powder

1½ teaspoons rice vinegar

⅔ cup (160 ml) canola oil

Pinch of kala namak

Anko Red Bean Paste

Season Year–round
Prep Time 30 minutes
Cook Time 3½ hours
Makes about ¾ cup (250 g)

Anko, a sweet red bean paste, is made from adzuki beans that have been simmered in sugar water for hours. There are two types: koshi-an, which is smooth, and tsubu-an, which is chunky. Bringing the beans to a boil and then rinsing them thoroughly several times helps to remove their bitterness. The paste takes quite a long time to prepare (4 hours), so I recommend making a large batch and freezing it.

1. Add the beans to a large pot along with enough water to cover by 1 inch (2.5 cm).

2. Bring the water to a boil over high heat. Remove the pot from the heat, drain, and then rinse the beans thoroughly.

3. Add the beans back to the pot along with enough water to cover by 1 inch (2.5 cm), and bring to a boil over high heat again. Let the beans boil for a few minutes, then drain and rinse the beans thoroughly. Repeat this step 3 to 4 more times. (The repeated boiling, draining, and rinsing removes the bitterness.)

4. After draining the beans for the last time, add enough water (preferably filtered) to cover by 1 inch (2.5 cm) once more, then cover the pot and cook over medium heat for 3 hours.

5. Once the beans are tender (you can easily squish them between your fingers), reserve ½ cup (120 ml) of the cooking water, then drain.

6. Return the reserved cooking water and beans to the pot, add the sugar, and stir the mixture over medium heat until the sugar has dissolved. Reduce the heat and continue cooking, stirring occasionally, until the liquid reduces and becomes creamy, about 30 minutes.

7. Turn off the heat and add the salt. If you would like chunky anko (known as *tsubu-an*), the paste is ready. If you prefer a smoother paste (known as *koshi-an*), use an immersion blender to blend it until the desired texture is achieved.

8. Store the paste in an airtight container in the refrigerator for 2 to 3 days, or freeze it for up to 2 months.

NOTE: You can find dried red adzuki beans at Asian markets or online.

½ cup (100 g) dried red adzuki beans (see Note)

¼ cup plus 2 tablespoons (75 g) sugar

Pinch of sea salt

MAIN DISHES

9月

日	月	火	水	木	金	土
					1	2
3	4	5	6	7	8	9
10	11	12	13	14	15	16
17	18	19	20	21	22	23
24	25	26	27	28	29	30

11

Curry Rice

Season Fall/Winter
Prep Time 20 minutes
Cook Time 25 minutes
Serves 3 to 4

Curry was brought to Japan by the English in the nineteenth century, during the Meiji era. Since then, it's become such a popular yōshoku dish that it is no longer considered Western, in fact, becoming a national dish. The Japanese version is sweeter than a traditional Indian curry, almost sugary. It starts with a roux of flour and butter to which lots of spices are added along with a sweetener like honey, apples, or sometimes a bit of dark chocolate. Here, I call for curry roux cubes—cubes of flour, fat, and spices—to thicken the dish and add flavor without the hassle of making a roux from scratch. Then potatoes, carrots, onions, and sometimes meat are added to the sauce. The curry can be topped with whatever you like: tonkatsu (fried cutlets), Korokke (stuffed croquettes; page 112), or vegetables.

1. Add the oil, onions, and salt to a large pot and sauté over medium heat until the onions are translucent, about 10 minutes. Add the applesauce, garlic, and ginger and sauté for a few minutes, then reduce the heat to medium-low, add the potatoes and carrot, and cook for a few minutes longer, until the vegetables are golden.

2. Add just enough water to cover the vegetables and bring to a boil over high heat. Reduce the heat to low and add the tomato sauce, soy sauce, curry cubes, and bay leaves. Stir until the curry cubes are completely dissolved, then add the cream, butter, and tonkatsu sauce.

3. Simmer for about 10 minutes, then remove the bay leaves. You can adjust the consistency of the curry by adding water to thin it, or by simmering longer to thicken it.

4. To serve, fill half a shallow bowl with the rice, then pour the curry into the other half.

NOTE: Prepared curry cubes are easy to find in any Asian market; I like the ones made by S&B and Java.

2 tablespoons canola oil

2 onions, chopped

2 pinches of salt

2 tablespoons unsweetened applesauce

2 garlic cloves, crushed

½ teaspoon grated ginger

2 potatoes, peeled and chopped

1 carrot, peeled and chopped

2 tablespoons tomato sauce (passata)

2 tablespoons soy sauce

3 curry roux cubes (see Note)

2 bay leaves

1 tablespoon plus 2 teaspoons vegan cream

1 tablespoon vegan butter

1 tablespoon tonkatsu sauce

2⅔ cups (500 g) cooked Japanese rice (page 7)

Hōtō

Season Winter
Prep time 10 minutes
Rest Time 20 minutes
Cook Time 5 minutes
Serves 4

Hōtō comes from the Yamanashi region and is composed of flat wheat udon noodles and vegetables in a miso broth. It's a comforting dish that is perfect for winter and rich in vitamins and minerals that help the immune system function properly. Hōtō is typically prepared with onions, leeks, potatoes, carrots, and Chinese cabbage, but you can add any vegetables you like. My favorite combination is daikon, kabocha squash, carrot, and leek. If you are using dried shiitakes, rehydrate them in a small bowl of hot water for about 20 minutes before slicing them.

1. Add the dashi (reserving a small amount), daikon, kabocha, leek, aburaage, carrot, shiitake, sake, mirin, and ginger to a large thick-bottomed saucepan over medium heat. Cover the pan, bring to a simmer, and simmer for 5 minutes.

2. Meanwhile, add the miso and the reserved dashi to a bowl and stir until the miso is completely dissolved.

3. Pour the miso mixture into the pan. Adjust the seasoning of the broth to taste by adding more miso or diluting with water.

4. To serve, add a portion of the noodles to a bowl, then top with a few ladles of soup, arranging some of the vegetables and the tofu on top, and garnish with shichimi togarashi.

1 recipe Kombu Dashi (page 14)

¼ daikon, peeled and cut crosswise into ¼-inch (6 mm) slices

¼ kabocha squash, peeled, seeded, and chopped

1 leek, rinsed and chopped

3 pieces aburaage, cut into ¼-inch (6 mm) slices

½ carrot, peeled and chopped

2 small shiitake mushrooms (fresh or dried), cut into ¼-inch (6 mm) slices

2 tablespoons plus 2 teaspoons sake

2 tablespoons mirin

1 teaspoon grated ginger

¼ cup plus 2 tablespoons (100 g) white miso

1 recipe Udon Noodles (page 25)

Shichimi togarashi

Mizore Nabe

Season Winter
Prep Time 20 minutes
Cook Time 20 minutes
Serves 4

Nabe is a classic Japanese winter stew. It is a social and comforting dish that is prepared in a donabe, or clay pot, and placed in the middle of the table to be shared. There are many kinds: kimchi nabe; anko nabe, with fugu (puffer fish); ishikari nabe, with salmon; chanko nabe, which is very popular among sumo wrestlers; mizutaki nabe, with chicken; or mizore nabe, with daikon. I like to use oat milk to make the broth rich and creamy. If you'd like to make the nabe look pretty, you can use a small cookie cutter to cut the carrot rounds into flower shapes.

1. Use a paring knife to cut a large star into the cap of the shiitake mushroom, being careful not to go all the way through, then set aside.

2. **To make the broth,** pour the two dashi broths into a donabe or large pot and bring to a boil over medium heat.

3. Reduce the heat to low and add the milk, sake, and ginger. Do not allow the broth to come to a boil.

4. Add the miso and whisk until it has dissolved completely.

5. **To make the nabe,** add the daikon and carrot to the broth. Cover and simmer over low heat for 5 minutes, then add the enoki and shimeji mushrooms, the firm tofu and the aburaage, and the cabbage, bok choy, and leek, and cook for another 10 minutes. Add the scallion, then remove from the heat.

6. Garnish the donabe or serving bowl with the shiitake before serving.

1 large fresh shiitake mushroom

BROTH

1½ cups (360 ml) Kombu Dashi (page 14)

1½ cups (360 ml) Shiitake Dashi (page 14)

2 cups plus 2 tablespoons (510 ml) oat milk

¼ cup (60 ml) sake

2 teaspoons grated ginger

¼ cup (70 g) red miso

NABE

½ daikon, peeled and cut into ⅛-inch (3 mm) rounds

1 small carrot, peeled and cut into ⅛-inch (3 mm) rounds

1 cup (250 g) enoki mushrooms, trimmed but left in a bunch

½ cup (100 g) shimeji mushrooms, trimmed but left in a bunch

10.5 ounces (300 g) firm tofu, chopped

4 pieces aburaage, chopped

¼ Chinese cabbage, cut into 2-inch (5 cm) slices

½ bok choy, cut into 2-inch (5 cm) slices

1 small leek, sliced on the bias

1 scallion, thinly sliced on the bias

Tantanmen

Season Winter
Prep Time 10 minutes
Cook Time 15 minutes
Serves 2

Whenever I'm enjoying a bowl of ramen, whether it's a spicy tantanmen at a restaurant or an instant version at home, it always makes me happy. I still remember the first time I tasted it: My mother had taken me to a tiny ramen *yasan*, a specialty restaurant, which smelled of the sweat of the workers who stopped in for a quick meal on their short lunch break. The tables were still dirty and my hands stuck to them as we sat on small stools, waiting for our food amidst the room's commotion, punctuated by greetings of "irasshaimase" welcoming new customers. Then, after a few minutes, huge bowls of ramen arrived under our noses. I tasted the soup first, then the noodles, then the toppings, and discovered an explosion of complementary flavors and textures. Today, ramen is a true treat that I can't go without!

1. Add the canola oil and tofu to a skillet over medium heat and fry until golden, about 5 minutes, then set aside.

2. Bring a medium pot of water to a boil over high heat, then add the bok choy leaves. Cook for 2 minutes, then drain and immediately rinse with cold water to blanch. Set aside.

3. Mix the miso, sesame oil, kombu dashi powder, garlic, peanut butter, ginger, and ¼ cup (60 ml) water together in a small bowl.

4. Heat the milk in a small saucepan over low heat until steaming; don't let it come to a boil. Pour the miso mixture into the hot milk and stir to combine.

5. Bring a large pot of water to a boil over high heat. Add the noodles and cook according to package instructions, then drain.

6. To serve, divide the noodles and milk mixture between two bowls. Garnish with the fried smoked tofu, cooked bok choy leaves, sliced scallions, sesame seeds, and a drizzle of rayu oil, and enjoy.

NOTE: There are many varieties of ramen broth, and each is eaten with a specific type of noodle: straight, curly, thin, or thick. Tantanmen is traditionally made with straight, thin noodles, but I personally prefer curly noodles, which hold on to some of the broth as you eat. Fresh ramen noodles often contain egg, so check the ingredients carefully; vegan ramen noodles can be found at some Asian markets, but if you can't find them, you can use instant ramen noodles instead.

1 tablespoon plus 2 teaspoons canola oil

5.5 ounces (160 g) smoked firm tofu, crumbled

4 bok choy leaves

3 tablespoons red miso

1 tablespoon plus 2 teaspoons toasted sesame oil

1 tablespoon plus 1 teaspoon kombu dashi powder

2 teaspoons grated garlic

1 teaspoon natural peanut butter

¾ teaspoon grated ginger

2½ cups (540 ml) soy milk

6.5 ounces (180 g) fresh ramen noodles (see Note)

GARNISH

Sliced scallions

Sesame seeds

Rayu chile oil

Miso Butter Ramen

Season Winter
Prep Time 5 minutes
Cook Time 15 minutes
Serves 2

Miso Butter Ramen is one of my favorite dishes to eat in the winter. Like the name suggests, it is made with a miso-based broth and topped with butter. We could of course substitute vegan butter to veganize this recipe, but here I use coconut oil because it is richer. Use a flavorless coconut oil to avoid changing the taste of the broth.

1. **To make the broth,** mix the coconut oil, miso, garlic, and dashi together in a small bowl. Divide the liquid evenly between two bowls.

2. Bring a large pot of water to a boil over high heat. Add the noodles to the pot and cook according to package instructions. Reserve 1¾ cups (420 ml) water, then drain the noodles. Divide the noodles between the bowls.

3. Divide the reserved water between the bowls and stir to combine with the noodles and broth. Garnish with the scallions, bamboo shoots, corn, mushrooms, and nori, and serve.

NOTES: Fresh ramen noodles often contain egg, so check the ingredients carefully; vegan ramen noodles can be found at some Asian markets, but if you can't find them, you can use instant ramen noodles instead.

Wood ear mushrooms can be found at Asian markets.

BROTH

3 tablespoons refined coconut oil

2 tablespoons plus 1 teaspoon red miso

1 tablespoon plus 2 teaspoons grated garlic

1 tablespoon Kombu Dashi (page 14)

6.5 ounces (180 g) fresh ramen noodles (see Notes)

GARNISH

2 scallions, thinly sliced on the bias

2 tablespoons bamboo shoots

2 tablespoons corn

6 wood ear mushrooms (see Notes)

½ nori sheet, cut into 2 pieces

Omuraisu

Season Spring
Prep Time 20 minutes
Cook Time 10 minutes
Serves 2

Omuraisu is a yōshoku dish that is loved by children and often found on the menu in famiresu restaurants. It's made by sautéing rice in ketchup and wrapping it in an omelet (*omu* means "omelet" and *raisu* means "rice"). This version, inspired by my mom's omuraisu, has a rice and tomato sauce base and tops the omelet with demi-glace sauce (but you can always use ketchup if you're feeling nostalgic!). I add onions and mushrooms to my recipe for more texture, but it's up to you. Using day-old rice gives the dish a better texture than freshly cooked rice, because it will have lost a bit of water.

1. **To make the omelet,** combine the soy milk, silken tofu, chickpea flour, sugar, dashi powder, baking powder, kala namak, and turmeric in a blender and blend on low speed just until smooth.

2. Heat a nonstick skillet over medium-high heat. Pour a large ladleful of the tofu mixture over the bottom to form a thin omelet. Cook for 1 to 2 minutes, then transfer the omelet to a plate. Repeat to make a second omelet.

3. **To make the rice filling,** add the smoked tofu and half of the chopped onion to the empty skillet with 1 teaspoon of the oil and sauté over medium heat until the onion is translucent, 8 to 10 minutes. Add the rice and stir well to separate the grains. Add the ketchup and soy sauce, and season with salt. Turn off the heat and set the skillet aside.

4. **To make the sauce,** add the remaining oil and onion to a saucepan and sauté over medium heat, for about 10 minutes, until golden. Add the mushrooms and sauté for 2 minutes, until softened. Stir in the demi-glace sauce, reduce the heat to low, and cook for a couple of minutes to warm through.

5. Place one of the omelets on a plate. Fill the omelet with the fried rice and fold the edges of the omelet over like a burrito to cover the filling completely. Repeat with the second omelet.

6. Remove the mushroom sauce from the heat and pour it over the omelets, then serve.

OMELET

1 cup (240 ml) soy milk

9 ounces (250 g; about 1 cup) silken tofu

½ cup (50 g) chickpea flour

1 teaspoon sugar

1 teaspoon kombu dashi powder

¼ teaspoon baking powder

Pinch of kala namak

Pinch of turmeric

RICE

1.75 ounces (50 g; about 3 tablespoons) smoked firm tofu, chopped

1 onion, chopped

2 teaspoons canola oil

1½ cups (300 g) day-old cooked Japanese rice (page 7)

¼ cup (70 g) ketchup

1 tablespoon soy sauce

SAUCE

1 ounce (30 g) shimeji or button mushrooms

⅓ cup (75 ml) Demi-Glace Sauce (page 19) or ketchup

Bento

Season Spring
Prep Time 1 hour
Cook Time 10 minutes
Serves 2

What I love about bento is that it is, all at once, beautiful, balanced, practical, *and* satisfying, and is even served cold. Children commonly carry it to school in their backpacks for lunch, and the most ambitious Japanese moms make their children kyaraben, elaborate packed lunches featuring foods made to look like cartoon characters (*kyara* for "character" and *ben* for "bento"). Of course, bentos are not only for children. They are also sold premade in konbinis, or 24-7 supermarkets. Bento come in as many varieties as you can imagine; this version, with karaage, broccoli, potato salad, tomatoes, and umeboshi plums, is my favorite.

1. Bring a medium pot of water to a boil over high heat. Add the broccoli and cook for 1 minute, then rinse immediately with cold water to blanch. Set aside.

2. Fill half a bento box with half of the rice. Place 1 heaping tablespoon of the potato salad, half of the broccoli, 2 or 3 pieces of the karaage, and 2 of the tomato halves in distinct piles in the empty space. Fill any remaining space with renkon and parsley, then top the rice with 1 umeboshi. Repeat with the second bento and serve.

¼ broccoli head, cut into florets

1½ cups (300 g) cooked Japanese rice (page 7)

2 heaping tablespoons Potato Salad (page 92)

4 to 6 karaage (page 83)

2 cherry tomatoes, halved

Renkon Sunomono (page 84)

Curly parsley

2 umeboshi plums

Oinari-San

Season Spring
Prep Time 30 minutes
Cook Time 20 minutes
Serves 3 to 4

Oinari-san, or inarizushi, is a traditional type of sushi made of aburaage (small pouches of deep-fried tofu) that's been stuffed with rice. In the simple Kanto-style version the inari are stuffed with rice and then wrapped like parcels in the tofu. In the Osaka-style version, the stuffed aburaage are open and garnished with colorful toppings. To celebrate the arrival of spring, I like to garnish my Osaka-style oinari-san with colorful edamame, seaweed caviar, edible flowers, and beni shoga (pickled ginger).

1. Cook the rice according to the instructions on page 7.

2. Add 1 tablespoon of the oil and the smoked tofu to a skillet over high heat and sauté until golden, about 5 minutes. Reduce the heat to low, add the teriyaki sauce, stir, and simmer until the sauce has thickened, 1 to 2 minutes. Transfer to a bowl and set aside.

3. Add the remaining tablespoon of oil and the firm tofu to the now-empty skillet over high heat and sauté until golden, about 5 minutes. Add the cream and stir until the tofu has absorbed the liquid, 2 to 4 minutes. Add the kala namak, salt, and turmeric. Stir to combine, then transfer to a second bowl and set aside.

4. Heat the aburaage in the empty skillet over low heat for 2 minutes. (The heat will help the pockets open more easily.) Remove the aburaage from the pan and squeeze them gently to release some of the liquid and to open their pockets. Set aside.

5. Add the rice and rice vinegar to a large bowl and stir to combine. (If the rice is still hot from cooking, let it cool just enough to handle.)

6. Holding an aburaage in your hand, use your other hand to fill it with rice. Pack the rice well but do not fill the pocket all the way to the top to ensure there's enough space for the toppings. Place the aburaage open-side up on a plate and repeat with the remaining aburaage and rice.

7. Top each oinari-san with both tofu mixtures. Garnish with the edamame and the seaweed caviar, beni shoga, and edible flowers, if using, and serve.

NOTE: You can find aburaage and beni shoga at Asian markets. Seaweed caviar is available at some vegan markets and specialty food stores.

3 cups (600 g) Japanese rice

2 tablespoons canola oil

4.5 ounces (125 g) smoked firm tofu, crumbled

2 tablespoons Teriyaki Sauce (page 23)

4.5 ounces (125 g) firm tofu

3 tablespoons vegan cream

2 pinches of kala namak

Pinch of salt

Pinch of turmeric

12 pieces aburaage

2 tablespoons rice vinegar

3 tablespoons shelled edamame

3 tablespoons seaweed caviar, optional

Beni shoga (pickled ginger), optional

Edible flowers, optional

Chahan

Season *Spring*
Prep Time *10 minutes*
Cook Time *10 minutes*
Serves *2*

Chahan is a traditional Chinese fried rice dish that made its way to Japan in the 1860s. It is eaten both in restaurants and at home, and it's very convenient because you can prepare it with leftovers from the day before. In fact, it will be even better when made with day-old rice because it will be firmer. You can add anything you want: vegetables, mushrooms, or tofu. This version is incredibly simple but reliable, inspired by my mother's recipe, which is seasoned with garlic. Feel free to add whatever additional ingredients you like, whether you want to clean out your refrigerator or simply satisfy a craving.

1. Heat a skillet over medium heat. Add the canola oil, onion, tofu, garlic, and chile, and sauté until golden, about 5 minutes.

2. Add the rice and stir with a spatula to prevent the grains from sticking to the bottom of the pan. Once the rice is warmed, 5 to 7 minutes, add the sesame oil and soy sauce, then season with salt.

3. Transfer half of the rice mixture to a medium bowl, pressing to pack it down. Place a plate on top and then, while holding them together, flip them over. Lift the bowl to reveal the rice, just as you would to remove a cake from a cake pan. Repeat with the remaining rice mixture.

4. Sprinkle the chopped scallions over the mounds of rice before serving.

2 tablespoons canola oil

½ onion, chopped

2 ounces (60 g) firm tofu, crumbled

4 garlic cloves, chopped

1 bird's-eye chile, stemmed, seeded, and cut into ⅛-inch (3 mm) slices

1½ cups (300 g) day-old cooked Japanese rice (page 7)

1 tablespoon toasted sesame oil

2 teaspoons soy sauce

1 scallion, chopped

Napolitan

Season Spring
Prep Time 15 minutes
Cook Time 25 minutes
Serves 2

I'm sure you're wondering why there is a spaghetti recipe in a Japanese cookbook! You might be surprised to learn that this dish is, in fact, a Japanese creation. The Napolitan, spaghetti sautéed in a sweet ketchup sauce with onions, peppers, and sausages, is a wafū pasta conception, a pasta dish that's been adjusted to suit Japanese tastes. It is often found in children's bentos and was one of my favorite meals when I was young. To make it a little more interesting for the grown-up palate (in Japanese we call this the *otona no aji*, or "adult taste"), I add roasted cherry tomatoes, red wine, and peppers.

1. Preheat the oven to 350°F (180°C). Line a baking sheet with parchment paper and arrange the cherry tomatoes on top. Drizzle with 1 tablespoon of the olive oil and season with coarse salt. Bake for 25 minutes, until softened.

2. Add the onions and remaining oil to a skillet and sauté over medium heat until the onions are translucent, 5 to 8 minutes, then add the bell peppers and hot dogs and sauté for a few minutes longer, until softened. Deglaze the pan with the red wine, then remove from the heat and set aside.

3. Bring a large pot filled with salted water to a boil over high heat. Add the pasta to the boiling water and cook for 8 to 10 minutes until al dente, then drain.

4. Add the ketchup, milk, soy sauce, Worcestershire sauce, and chile pepper to the skillet of sautéed vegetables and hot dogs. Return the skillet to medium heat and simmer until the liquid is slightly thickened, about 5 minutes. Add the spaghetti and tomatoes and stir to combine. Season with salt and pepper.

5. To serve, divide the spaghetti between two shallow bowls and garnish with the parsley.

- 8 cherry tomatoes
- 3 tablespoons olive oil
- ½ onion, thinly sliced
- 2 small green bell peppers, cut into ¼-inch (6 mm) slices
- 2 vegan hot dogs, chopped
- ¼ cup (60 ml) red wine
- 6.5 ounces (180 g) spaghetti
- ½ cup plus 2 tablespoons (150 ml) ketchup
- ¼ cup plus 2 tablespoons (90 ml) vegan milk
- 2 tablespoons soy sauce
- 2 tablespoons vegan Worcestershire sauce
- 1 bird's-eye chile, stemmed, seeded, and cut into ⅛-inch (3 mm) slices
- Curly parsley

Soboro Don

Season Spring
Prep Time 10 minutes
Cook Time 10 minutes
Serves 2

Soboro don is a very popular type of donburi (a large rice bowl with toppings) in Japan, enjoyed hot or at room temperature. *Soboro* means "ground," referring to the ground chicken that's typically used, and *don* is an abbreviation of donburi. It is also called *sanshoku don*, or "three-color donburi," because the rice is usually topped with chicken, scrambled eggs, and green vegetables. Here, I use plant-based meat and, to substitute the scrambled eggs, tofu with a little bit of kala namak.

1. Bring a medium pot of water to a boil over high heat. Add the komatsuna and cook for 2 minutes, then drain and rinse in cold water to blanch.

2. Add 1 teaspoon of the oil and ginger to a skillet over medium heat and sauté for 1 minute, then add the plant-based meat and cook according to the package instructions. Once the meat is well browned, reduce the heat, add the miso glaze to taste, and stir to combine. Transfer the meat mixture to a bowl and set aside.

3. Add the remaining oil and the tofu to the empty skillet and sauté over medium heat, until golden. Reduce the heat and add the cream, kala namak, salt, and turmeric. Simmer until the tofu has absorbed the cream, about 4 minutes.

4. To serve, divide the rice between two bowls. Arrange the toppings in long stripes: the komatsuna on top of one third of the rice, the ground meat on another third, and the scrambled tofu on the remaining third. Pour the ponzu sauce over the komatsuna and garnish with the beni shoga.

NOTE: Komatsuna can be found at Asian markets and some supermarkets. Beni shoga can also be found at Asian markets.

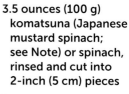

3.5 ounces (100 g) komatsuna (Japanese mustard spinach; see Note) or spinach, rinsed and cut into 2-inch (5 cm) pieces

2 teaspoons canola oil

½-inch (1.25 cm) piece ginger, cut into ⅛-inch (3 mm) slices

1⅓ cups (150 g) plant-based ground meat or rehydrated textured vegetable protein (TVP)

3 to 4 tablespoons Miso Glaze (page 20)

3.5 ounces (100 g) firm tofu, crumbled

3 tablespoons plus 1 teaspoon plant-based cream

2 pinches of kala namak

2 pinches of salt

Pinch of turmeric

1½ cups (300 g) cooked Japanese rice (page 7)

¼ cup (60 ml) Ponzu Sauce (page 17)

Beni shoga (pickled ginger)

Hiyashi Chūka

Season *Summer*
Prep Time *10 minutes*
Rest Time *10 minutes*
Cook Time *15 minutes*
Serves *2*

Cold dishes are the ideal antidote to Japan's hot summers. Salads are an obvious choice, but the Japanese love their noodles and make a cold version of all their favorites. Hiyashi chūka is like a chilled ramen: Both dishes use the same wheat-based noodles and are topped with vegetables and a sauce. The refreshing combination of tomato, cucumber, corn, and noodles is perfect for summer.

1. Add the cucumber to a colander set over a bowl, sprinkle it with the salt, and stir to evenly distribute it over the cucumber. Let the cucumber drain for about 10 minutes, then press firmly with your hands to squeeze out its excess water. Set aside.

2. Cook the noodles according to the package instructions, then immediately drain and rinse them with cold water to stop their cooking.

3. Divide the noodles between two shallow bowls and pour the vinaigrette on top. Top with the smoked tofu, tomato, nori, and corn, and serve.

NOTE: Fresh ramen noodles often contain egg, so check the ingredients carefully; vegan ramen noodles can be found at some Asian markets, but if you can't find them, you can use instant ramen noodles instead.

1/3 large cucumber, seeded and cut lengthwise into 1/4-inch (6 mm) slices

1 1/2 teaspoons salt

6.5 ounces (180 g) fresh ramen noodles (see Note)

Hiyashi Chūka Vinaigrette (page 23)

1.75 ounces (50 g; about 3 tablespoons) smoked firm tofu, cut into 1/4-inch (6 mm) slices

1 small beefsteak tomato, cut into 1/2-inch (1.25 cm) slices

One 4-inch (10 cm) square nori sheet, cut into strips

1/2 cup (70 g) canned corn

Maguro Don

Season Summer
Prep Time 10 minutes
Cook Time 35 minutes
Serves 2

Japan is surrounded by sea, so the country naturally has a developed fishing industry, and seafood is arguably the most important element of Japanese cuisine. You might think that it would be difficult to replicate the taste of the ocean in vegan cuisine, but plants will surprise you! Seaweed is a fairly obvious example, since it comes directly from the ocean and contains large amounts of iodine, a briny-tasting mineral. On dry land, there's the oyster plant which, as its name implies, has an oyster-like flavor. And as an even more astonishing example, avocado mixed with soy sauce tastes just like maguro, or Japanese tuna. I use all three of these to give this vegan version of maguro don, which is typically made with marinated tuna, its seafood flavor. For appearance and texture, I also use tender roasted red bell peppers.

1. Preheat the oven to 400°F (200°C) and line a baking sheet with parchment paper. Place the peppers on the sheet and roast for 35 minutes, flipping the peppers halfway through roasting.

2. Once cooked, seal the peppers in an airtight container and set in the refrigerator to cool. Once the peppers have cooled enough to handle, remove the skin, stem, and seeds. Cut each pepper into 8 to 10 square pieces.

3. Divide the rice between two bowls and top with the oyster plant leaves, if using, and some of the nori. Fan out the avocado over the entire surface of the rice, then fan out the pepper over the avocado. Drizzle with the soy sauce to taste, then garnish with the scallion, a sprinkle of sesame seeds, the remaining nori, and a bit of wasabi, if using. Serve.

NOTE: You can find oyster plant leaves at some specialty markets or online.

- 2 large red bell peppers
- 1¾ cups (350 g) cooked Japanese rice (page 7)
- 3 small oyster plant leaves, thinly sliced (see Note), optional
- 1 nori sheet, cut into ¼-inch (6 mm) slices
- 2 ripe avocados, pitted and cut into ¼-inch (6 mm) slices
- 3 to 4 tablespoons (45 to 60 ml) soy sauce
- 1 scallion, chopped
- White sesame seeds
- Wasabi, optional

Zaru Udon

Season Summer
Prep Time 10 minutes
Serves 2

Zaru udon—thick wheat-based udon noodles eaten with a soy-based dipping sauce called *mentsuyu*—is a rich yet refreshing summertime meal. It's normally seasoned with ground sesame seeds, grated daikon, and a little wasabi. The dish gets its name from zaru, the shallow bamboo basket traditionally used to serve it. There is also zaru soba, a version with soba (buckwheat) noodles. You can add tempura or fried vegetables to make the dish known as *tenzaru udon*.

1. Using a spice grinder or a mortar and pestle, grind the sesame seeds into a powder.

2. Add the sesame powder and the mentsuyu, daikon, and wasabi, if using, to a small bowl and stir to combine.

3. Serve the noodles on a zaru or a deep serving plate, topped with the mentsuyu mixture and the vegetable tempura, if using.

2 teaspoons sesame seeds

2 cups (480 ml) diluted chilled Mentsuyu (page 24)

One 2-inch (5 cm) piece daikon, peeled and finely grated

1 teaspoon wasabi, optional

14 ounces (400 g) cooked Udon Noodles (page 25)

1 recipe Tempura (page 131), optional

Miso Nasu Donburi

Season Summer
Prep Time 15 minutes
Cook Time 30 minutes
Serves 2

When I think of summer vegetables, the first one that comes to mind is eggplant (or *nasu* in Japanese). I love them in donburi (rice bowls with toppings), which are baked in the oven, glazed with miso, and served with high-quality Japanese white rice.

1. Preheat the oven to 400°F (200°C) and line a baking sheet with parchment paper.

2. Arrange the eggplant slices on the baking sheet and drizzle both sides evenly with the oil. They need to be entirely covered, so don't be afraid to pour generously. Roast for 30 minutes, until the eggplant flesh is soft and golden.

3. When the eggplant is done roasting, divide the rice between two bowls and arrange the eggplant slices on top. Drizzle with the miso glaze and sprinkle with the chopped scallions and sesame seeds, and serve.

NOTE: Japanese eggplants are smaller and more elongated and have softer skin than the globe eggplants found in many supermarkets. The amount of oil you'll need will depend on the size of your eggplants.

2 Japanese eggplants, cut lengthwise into ½-inch (1.25 cm) slices

½ to 1 cup (120–240 ml) canola oil

1½ cups (300 g) cooked Japanese rice (page 7)

2 to 3 tablespoons Miso Glaze (page 20)

1 scallion, thinly sliced on the bias

Toasted white sesame seeds

Kabocha Stew

Season *Fall*
Prep Time *15 minutes*
Cook Time *1 hour*
Serves *4*

Kabocha squash is one of Japan's most popular fall vegetables, and ever since I was a child, I've found kabocha stew to be one of the most comforting dishes to eat during the colder months. It is often served in famiresu, family-style restaurants serving Western dishes adapted to suit Japanese tastes. For a real taste of fall in Japan, the kabocha is worth seeking out.

1. Preheat the oven to 425°F (220°C). Wrap the squash in aluminum foil and roast for 40 to 50 minutes, until the squash is very tender.

2. Meanwhile, sauté the onions with the butter in a large pot over medium heat until tender and caramelized, about 20 minutes.

3. Bring a large pot of water to a boil over high heat. Add the carrot and cook for 2 minutes, then use a slotted spoon to remove it from the water and set aside. Add the broccoli to the boiling water, cook for 2 minutes, then drain and set aside.

4. Once the onions are caramelized, add the potato starch and stir to combine. Add the milk and bouillon cube and mix well, then use an immersion blender to puree the mixture. Add the kombu dashi powder and salt, stir, and adjust the salt to taste.

5. Add the tofu, broccoli, and carrots, bring to a simmer, and stir until the stew thickens slightly, 4 to 5 minutes.

6. Serve immediately.

2¾ cups (350 g) peeled and chopped kabocha squash

2 onions, chopped

2 tablespoons vegan butter or canola oil

1 small carrot, peeled and chopped

1 head broccoli, chopped

3 tablespoons potato starch or cornstarch

2 cups plus 2 tablespoons (510 ml) soy milk

1 vegetable bouillon cube

2 tablespoons kombu dashi powder

1 teaspoon salt

7 ounces (200 g) smoked tofu, cubed

Teriyaki Tofu Don

Season Fall
Prep Time 10 minutes
Cook Time 15 minutes
Serves 2

In Japan, tofu is most often eaten in its silken version, with just a hint of soy sauce. I discovered firm tofu only after becoming vegan. It's a great alternative to meat thanks to its chicken-like texture and its high protein content. I especially love it with a crispy potato starch coating and covered in teriyaki sauce.

1. Add 2 tablespoons of the canola oil and the chopped onion to a skillet and sauté over medium heat until the onion is translucent, about 5 minutes, then transfer it to a small bowl and set aside.

2. Combine the tofu and potato starch in a bowl. Stir well to coat the tofu pieces completely.

3. Sauté the tofu in the remaining canola oil in the empty skillet until the tofu turns crispy and golden brown, about 5 minutes. Drizzle with the sesame oil and add the onion, then reduce the heat to low and add the teriyaki sauce. Mix well.

4. Divide the rice between two bowls and top with the tofu mixture. Drizzle with the mayonnaise, if using, and sprinkle with the sesame seeds and microgreens before serving.

- ¼ cup (60 ml) canola oil
- 1 small onion, chopped
- 16 ounces (450 g) firm tofu, cubed
- ¼ cup (30 g) potato starch or cornstarch
- ½ teaspoon toasted sesame oil
- ⅓ cup (100 ml) Teriyaki Sauce (page 23)
- 1½ cups (300 g) cooked Japanese rice (page 7)
- Japanese Mayonnaise (page 29), optional
- 2 teaspoons white sesame seeds
- Pinch of daikon microgreens or 1 small chopped scallion

MAYO

Ramen with Soy Sauce and Garlic

One of the most classic types of ramen is made with shōyu broth. This soy sauce broth is traditionally made with chicken bones, but I substitute seaweed and coconut oil which adds the fatty richness that ramen is famous for.

Season *Fall*
Prep time *20 minutes*
Cook Time *1 hour*
Serves *2*

1. Preheat the oven to 350°F (180°C). Brush the garlic with the canola oil, wrap in aluminum foil, and roast for 1 hour, until soft.

2. While the garlic roasts, sauté the tofu with the sesame oil in a skillet over medium heat until golden brown, about 5 minutes, then transfer it to a bowl and set aside.

3. Sauté the bean sprouts in the empty skillet until tender, 4 to 5 minutes, then set aside.

4. Cook the noodles according to package instructions, then drain and divide between two bowls.

5. Bring 2½ cups (600 ml) water to a boil. Add the boiling water, kombu dashi powder, soy sauce, coconut oil, and roasted garlic to a blender and blend until smooth. Divide the broth between the bowls, garnish with the smoked tofu, bean sprouts, bamboo shoots, chopped scallions, and nori, and serve immediately.

NOTE: Fresh ramen noodles often contain egg, so check the ingredients carefully; vegan ramen noodles can be found at some Asian markets, but if you can't find them, you can use instant ramen noodles instead.

¼ cup (35 g) garlic cloves, peeled

2 tablespoons canola oil

3.5 ounces (100 g) smoked tofu, cut into ¼-inch (6 mm) slices

2 tablespoons toasted sesame oil

½ cup (50 g) bean sprouts

6.5 ounces (180 g) fresh ramen noodles (see Note)

1 tablespoon plus 2 teaspoons kombu dashi powder or 2½ cups (600 ml) homemade dashi (page 14)

2 tablespoons soy sauce

1 tablespoon plus 1 teaspoon refined coconut oil

GARNISH

12 bamboo shoots

1 chopped scallion

1 piece nori seaweed, cut in half

Mabo Dofu

Season Fall
Prep Time 20 minutes
Cook Time 5 minutes
Serves 2 to 3

Like bitterness, spice is a taste that took me a while to appreciate. We say that taste changes with age, which was certainly true for me; I went from craving sweet foods to craving spice. I now put hot sauce on just about everything and I love discovering new spices. Two of my favorite spicy ingredients are gochujang and Sichuan peppercorns, from Korea and China respectively. Mabo dofu (or mapo tofu) came to Japan from China, and it's the dish I turn to when I'm craving spice and heat. Traditionally, it is prepared with large pieces of tofu, beef, and a fiery Sichuan pepper sauce. In the Japanese version, the sauce is a little sweeter and the dish is usually served with rice.

1. **To make the sauce,** combine the doubanjiang, sesame oil, mirin, sugar, black bean paste, chile crisp, soy sauce, and gochujang in a small bowl. In a second small bowl, mix the cold water and potato starch. Pour the contents of the second bowl into the first and stir to combine.

2. **To make the stew,** add the canola oil, garlic, ginger, and half of the scallions to a skillet over medium heat and sauté for about 90 seconds, until fragrant, then add the plant-based ground meat and cook for a couple of minutes, until golden and crispy.

3. Reduce the heat to low, add the sauce, and stir to combine. Gently add the tofu. Cook just long enough to warm the tofu, 3 to 4 minutes, then remove from the heat. (Do not leave the sauce on the heat for too long or it will become overly concentrated and salty. Add water to dilute if needed.)

4. Divide the mabo dofu between deep bowls, then sprinkle with the sesame seeds and the remaining chopped scallion. Place a small pile of togarashi threads on top and serve immediately with the rice.

NOTE: I recommend doubanjiang, black bean paste, and chile crisp made by Laoganma; this brand is easily found in Asian markets and offers vegan versions of their sauces. Ito togarashi can be found at Asian markets.

SAUCE

1 tablespoon plus 2 teaspoons doubanjiang (see Note)

1 tablespoon plus 2 teaspoons toasted sesame oil

1 tablespoon mirin

1 tablespoon sugar

2¼ teaspoons black bean paste

2 teaspoons chile crisp

1 teaspoon soy sauce

½ teaspoon gochujang

½ cup (120 ml) cold water

1½ teaspoons potato starch or cornstarch

STEW

1 tablespoon plus 2 teaspoons canola oil

2 garlic cloves, chopped

One 1-inch (2.5 cm) piece ginger, chopped

2 scallions, chopped

1 cup (100 g) plant-based ground meat or rehydrated textured vegetable protein (TVP)

8 ounces (230 g) silken or firm tofu, cubed

GARNISH

1 teaspoon white sesame seeds

2 pinches ito togarashi chile threads

1½ cups (300 g) cooked Japanese rice (page 7)

Kitsune Udon

Season Fall/Winter
Prep Time 10 minutes
Cook Time 15 minutes
Serves 2

Kitsune means "fox" in Japanese. There are several theories as to why this dish is named after the animal. In Japanese folklore, aburaage (fried tofu) is often said to be a fox's favorite food. Some people believe it's because the golden color of the tofu is reminiscent of the animal's coat. One thing is sure: Kitsune udon is one of the most popular dishes in Japan and is served hot during the winter as often as it is served cold during the summer.

1. Bring about 2 cups (240 ml) water to a boil. Divide the mentsuyu between 2 bowls and dilute each with ⅓ to ⅔ cups (80–160 ml) of the boiling water, depending on how concentrated you wish the broth to be.

2. Divide the noodles between the bowls. Top with the aburaage, scallion, daikon, and shichimi togarashi, and serve immediately.

¼ cup plus
 3 tablespoons
 (100 ml) concentrated
 Mentsuyu (page 24)

14 ounces (400 g)
 cooked Udon Noodles
 (page 25)

4 pieces aburaage, cut
 in half

1 scallion, chopped

One 2-inch (5 cm) piece
 daikon, peeled and
 finely grated

2 teaspoons shichimi
 togarashi

Miso Soup

Season Winter
Prep Time 10 minutes
Cook Time 10 minutes
Serves 3 to 4

Miso soup is an essential part of a complete Japanese meal. Personally, I love this soup because it is both deeply comforting and very healthy thanks to the probiotic-rich fermented miso. I usually add silken tofu, wakame seaweed, and sesame paste for extra depth and richness, but you can also bulk it up with vegetables like potatoes or daikon. Miso varies in flavor and saltiness by brand; adjust the seasoning of your soup by tasting it and adding more miso or water depending on your tastes.

1. Combine the two broths in a medium pot and warm over medium heat. Add the tofu, ginger, and wakame, and allow the wakame to rehydrate, about 5 minutes.

2. Reduce the heat to low and ladle a small portion of the broth into a small bowl. Add the miso and sesame paste to the bowl and stir gently until completely dissolved and smooth, then pour the miso mixture back into the pot and stir to combine.

3. Remove the ginger from the pot before serving.

¾ cup plus
  1 tablespoon (200 ml)
  Kombu Dashi
  (page 14)

¾ cup plus
  1 tablespoon (200 ml)
  Shiitake Dashi
  (page 14)

6.5 ounces (180 g)
  silken tofu, cubed

One ¾-inch (2 cm)
  piece ginger

2 pinches of dried
  wakame

¼ cup plus
  1 tablespoon (80 g)
  red miso

1 teaspoon white
  sesame paste or
  tahini

Nikujaga

Season Winter
Prep Time 15 minutes
Cook Time 35 minutes
Serves 3 to 4

Nikujaga is the Japanese version of an English stew; *niku* means "meat" and *jaga* is an abbreviation of *jagaimo*, which means "potato." Invented in the nineteenth century, this is one of the very first yōshoku dishes, and it's easy to make vegan by substituting textured vegetable protein for the meat! It's one of my favorite Japanese comfort foods because it is all at once healthy, delicious, and warming, yet light enough to be enjoyed alongside soup and rice. The secret to its irresistibility lies in the savory dashi and the balance between the salty soy sauce and the sweet mirin. This dish tastes even better the next day.

1. Rehydrate the TVP in 3¾ cups (900 ml) water. Once the protein has tripled in volume and most of the water is absorbed, drain and squeeze it with your hands to release the extra liquid.

2. Add the oil and onions to a large pot over high heat and cook until the onions begin to brown, about 10 minutes. Add the salt and reduce the heat to medium, cover the skillet with a lid, and continue to cook, stirring occasionally, until the onions caramelize, about 10 minutes.

3. Add the potatoes, carrot, noodles, and vegetable protein to the pot. Sauté for about 3 minutes, until just starting to turn golden, then add the soy sauce, mirin, sake, sugar, kombu dashi powder, and 1¾ cups (420 ml) water.

4. Turn up the heat to bring to a boil. Use a slotted spoon to skim the foam that will form on the surface. Reduce the heat and cover. Simmer for 20 minutes.

5. Meanwhile, bring a small pot of water to a boil, add the snow peas, and cook for 4 to 5 minutes, until tender, then drain and cut the snow peas in half lengthwise.

6. When the sauce has almost completely reduced and the potatoes are tender, turn off the heat and leave the pot covered for an additional 10 minutes. Adjust the seasoning to taste with extra water or soy sauce.

7. Divide the nikujaga between shallow bowls, arranging the snow peas on top, and serve.

- 1¼ cups (80 g) textured vegetable protein (TVP)
- 3 tablespoons canola oil
- 2 large onions, sliced
- 2 pinches of salt
- 4 to 5 large potatoes, peeled and chopped
- 1 large carrot, peeled and chopped
- One 7-ounce (200 g) pack shirataki (konjac) noodles, rinsed
- ¼ cup plus 2 tablespoons (90 ml) soy sauce
- ¼ cup (60 ml) mirin
- ¼ cup (60 ml) sake
- ¼ cup (50 g) sugar
- 1 tablespoon kombu dashi powder
- 12 snow peas

Corn Soup

Season *Winter*
Prep Time *5 minutes*
Cook Time *25 minutes*
Serves *2 to 3*

As its name suggests, corn soup (pronounced "konn supu" by the Japanese) is not a traditional Japanese soup. This yōshoku dish was imported from England and is often prepared at home from freeze-dried packets or eaten in famiresu restaurants. Slightly sweet and very rich, this nostalgic soup evokes childhood memories for many.

1. Add the butter and onion to a medium saucepan over medium heat and sauté until the onions are caramelized, at least 20 minutes.

2. Meanwhile, add the hot water and bouillon cube to a small bowl and stir until dissolved.

3. Once the onions are caramelized, add the flour and stir constantly for about 3 minutes to cook off its raw flavor.

4. Reduce the heat and add the bouillon mixture, then the corn. Use an immersion blender to blend until smooth.

5. Strain the mixture through a fine-mesh strainer into another pot to remove any chunks.

6. Add the milk, salt, kombu dashi powder, and pepper. Heat over medium until the mixture is warm, about 3 minutes, and adjust the salt to taste, then serve.

2 tablespoons vegan butter or canola oil

1 onion, chopped

1 cup (240 ml) hot water

1 vegetable bouillon cube

¼ cup (30 g) flour

1½ cups (9 oz/250 g) canned corn

1½ cups (360 ml) oat or soy milk

1 teaspoon salt

½ teaspoon kombu dashi powder

2 pinches of pepper

Karaage

Season *Winter*
Prep Time *10 minutes*
Rest Time *15 minutes*
Chill Time *12 hours*
Cook Time *10 minutes*
Serves *2*

Karaage is Japanese fried chicken that is marinated overnight in a mixture of soy sauce, sugar, and garlic, then coated in potato starch and fried. It is a very popular side dish in Japan, especially in bentos. It can be served with mayonnaise for richness, or lightened with lemon juice. Textured vegetable protein chunks or medallions imitate chicken well.

1. Soak the TVP chunks in three times their volume of water for at least 15 minutes to rehydrate. Once they have absorbed most of the water, squeeze by hand to drain the excess.

2. Add the vegetable protein, sake, soy sauce, sugar, sesame oil, and garlic to a large ziplock plastic bag and knead gently to mix. Seal the bag tightly and marinate overnight in the refrigerator.

3. The next day, remove the vegetable protein from the bag and squeeze gently to remove the excess marinade.

4. Combine the flour, potato starch, and shichimi togarashi, if using, in a bowl, add the vegetable protein, and mix until it is evenly coated.

5. Warm the oil in a large pot over medium-high heat. Once the oil has reached 320 to 340°F (160–170°C), gently add the vegetable protein chunks and fry until the crust is golden, 3 to 5 minutes. (If you don't have a thermometer, you can test the oil by adding a small piece of vegetable protein; if it sizzles immediately, the oil is ready.) Using a slotted spoon or spider skimmer, remove the karaage from the oil and place them on a cooling rack or colander lined with paper towels to soak up the excess oil.

6. Serve warm with the mayonnaise.

NOTE: You can find textured vegetable protein chunks or medallions at Asian markets and some specialty vegan markets or health food stores. Don't use small strips or curls of TVP here; these are not the right shape and size for karaage.

Ingredients

- 8 to 10 textured vegetable protein (TVP) chunks or medallions (see Note)
- ¼ cup (60 ml) sake
- ¼ cup (60 ml) soy sauce
- ¼ cup (50 g) sugar
- 1 tablespoon toasted sesame oil
- 2 garlic cloves, grated
- 2 tablespoons flour
- 1 tablespoon plus 2 teaspoons potato starch or cornstarch
- 1 teaspoon shichimi togarashi, optional
- ¾ cup (180 ml) sunflower or canola oil
- Japanese Mayonnaise (page 29) or lemon juice

Pickled Lotus Root
(Renkon Sunomono)

Season Winter
Prep Time 10 minutes
Rest Time 15 minutes
Chill Time 12 hours See step 4.
Cook Time 1 minute
Serves 2

I adore renkon, or lotus root, because of its crisp texture and health benefits, but especially because it can be prepared in a myriad of different ways. One of my favorites is as a pickle, or sunomono. In Japan, renkon sunomono is often prepared as part of *osechi*, a sort of traditional New Year's Eve bento, because it brings good fortune, and we say that you can see the future through the renkon's holes.

1. Cut V-shaped notches between each hole along the outer length of the renkon. Continue cutting around the contour of the holes to form the shape of a flower, then cut the renkon into very thin slices.

2. Add the slices to a large bowl of cold water and let stand for about 10 minutes, then drain the water.

3. Add the sugar, vinegar, and salt to a small pot and bring to a boil over high heat. Reduce the heat to medium and boil for 1 minute, then turn off the heat. Add the kombu and let cool.

4. Transfer the renkon to a storage container and pour the cold vinegar mixture on top. Add the yuzu zest, if using, and then seal the container and let the renkon marinate in the refrigerator for 12 hours.

5. Remove the kombu before serving. If you have any leftovers you would like to save, I recommend pouring out the marinade so that the renkon doesn't become too saturated. The renkon can then be stored in an airtight container in the refrigerator for up to 3 days.

NOTE: If you can't find fresh renkon, look for frozen, presliced renkon in Asian markets. If you are using frozen renkon, soak the slices in hot water for 10 minutes to thaw before trimming each slice into a flower shape.

One 2-inch (5 cm) piece renkon (lotus root; see Note)

2 tablespoons sugar

¾ cup plus 1 tablespoon (200 ml) rice vinegar

2 pinches salt

One 4-inch (10 cm) square kombu sheet

1 pinch yuzu zest, optional

Kimchi

Season *Winter*
Prep Time *20 minutes*
Rest Time *4 to 4½ hours*
Cook Time *10 minutes*
Fermentation Time *5 days*
Makes about *4½ pounds (2 kg) kimchi*

Kimchi is a traditional Korean side dish that is widely consumed in Japan today. Many Japanese kimchi manufacturers skip the fermentation process, resulting in a version that's less acidic than Korean kimchi. Personally, I find that fermenting the kimchi adds a lot of flavor, so I recommend letting the mixture rest for a few days before enjoying! I also like to add a little applesauce to my version, for sweetness.

1. Add the cabbage and coarse salt to a large bowl. Mix by hand until all the cabbage leaves are completely coated in salt. Let stand at room temperature for 3 hours.

2. Check if the cabbage leaves are soft after 3 hours have passed. If they are still crisp, let stand for another 30 minutes.

3. Rinse the cabbage thoroughly in a colander under running water to remove the excess salt. Let it drain for at least 1 hour. Once dry, transfer the cabbage to a large bowl.

4. Add the cold water, mushrooms, and kombu to a pot and bring to a boil over high heat. As soon as the water begins to bubble, remove the kombu. Turn off the heat and let the mushrooms steep for 10 minutes. Remove the mushrooms and let the broth cool completely.

5. Once the broth has cooled, add the rice flour and mix well to break up any lumps. Return to a boil, whisking continuously until the mixture thickens, 2 to 3 minutes. Transfer to a bowl and add the garlic, ginger, fine salt, applesauce, and gochugaru. Puree the mixture with an immersion or stand blender.

6. Add the carrot, daikon, and scallion to the sauce and stir to combine. Pour the mixture into the bowl of cabbage, add the sesame seeds, and mix by hand. (Be careful, it's spicy! Wear gloves to protect your hands from the gochugaru.)

7. Transfer to an airtight container and ferment for 5 days at room temperature. Once fermented (the kimchi should smell slightly sour), move the airtight container to the refrigerator.

NOTE: Gochugaru, a Korean chile powder, is available at Asian markets.

- 1 Chinese cabbage (6.5 pounds/3 kg), cored, chopped, and rinsed
- ½ cup plus 1 tablespoon (130 g) coarse salt
- 1½ cups (360 ml) cold water
- 4 dried shiitake mushrooms
- One 5-inch (13 cm) square kombu sheet
- 1 tablespoon plus 2 teaspoons rice flour
- 4 garlic cloves
- One 4-inch (10 cm) piece ginger
- 1 teaspoon fine salt
- ¾ cup plus 2 teaspoons (200 g) applesauce
- ½ cup (125 g) gochugaru (see Note)
- 1 carrot, peeled and julienned
- 1 daikon (250 g), peeled and julienned
- 4 scallions, thinly sliced on the bias
- 2 tablespoons white sesame seeds, toasted

Hanbāgu

Season *Spring*
Prep Time *20 minutes*
Cook Time *10 minutes*
Makes *6 steaks*

Hanbāgu (not to be confused with hamburger) is one of the most classic yōshoku dishes. Often found on famiresu menus, it's a soft and juicy Japanese-style chopped steak served with a demi-glace sauce that pairs beautifully with rice and is equally good served cold as part of a bento. For a vegan version, I add mushrooms and tofu to plant-based meat to give it extra texture and flavor.

1. Add the oil, onions, and mushrooms to a skillet and sauté over medium heat until softened, 5 to 8 minutes.

2. Combine the plant-based meat, cubed tofu, silken tofu, and soy cream in a large bowl. Add the onions and shiitake mushrooms and mix well until combined. Add the flour, panko, kombu dashi powder, salt, and pepper, and stir to combine.

3. Form 6 balls, then press lightly to flatten. Heat a nonstick skillet over medium heat. Cook the steaks, covered, for about 5 minutes on each side.

4. To serve, top with the demi-glace sauce.

1 tablespoon plus 2 teaspoons canola oil

2 onions, finely chopped

4 fresh shiitake mushrooms, finely chopped

1 ⅓ cups (150 g) plant-based ground meat or rehydrated textured vegetable protein (TVP)

3.5 ounces (100 g) firm tofu, cubed

¼ cup (2 oz/60 g) silken tofu

3 tablespoons plus 2 teaspoons soy cream

⅓ cup (45 g) flour

¼ cup plus 1 tablespoon (20 g) panko

1¼ teaspoons kombu dashi powder

½ teaspoon salt

¼ teaspoon pepper

¼ cup (60 ml) Demi-Glace Sauce (page 19)

Hiyayakko
(Cold Tofu)

Season *Spring*
Prep Time *10 minutes*
Cook Time *5 minutes*
Chill Time *1 hour*
Serves *2*

In France, even the most seasoned vegans don't usually eat silken tofu plain; they're more likely to use it as an egg replacement in baking. In Japan, however, due to the high-quality soy available, the tofu is excellent, so it's common to eat silken tofu plain, with just a bit of soy sauce, as a refreshing and healthy side dish.

1. **To make the sauce,** add the mirin and sake to a small saucepan and bring to a boil over high heat. Reduce the heat and simmer for about 2 minutes to cook off the alcohol. Turn off the heat and add the soy sauce and kombu sheet. Let the mixture cool completely, then remove the kombu and chill in the refrigerator for at least 1 hour.

2. Add the ginger to the chilled sauce and stir to combine.

3. **To plate the hiyayakko,** arrange the blocks of tofu on plates and pour the desired amount of sauce on top. Garnish with the sliced scallion and a small scoop of the daikon puree. Sprinkle with the sesame seeds and finish with a small drizzle of the rayu oil, if using.

4. Serve chilled.

SAUCE

2 tablespoons plus 2 teaspoons mirin

2 teaspoons sake

½ cup plus 2 tablespoons (150 ml) soy sauce

One 2-inch (5 cm) square kombu sheet

HIYAYAKKO

One 1½-inch (4 cm) piece ginger, grated

10.5 ounces (300 g) silken tofu, cut into 2 pieces

1 scallion, sliced thinly on the bias

One 2-inch (5 cm) piece daikon, finely grated

2 teaspoons white sesame seeds, toasted

1 teaspoon rayu chile oil, optional

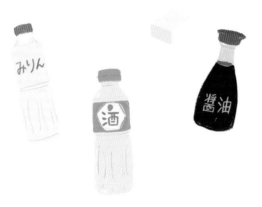

Japanese Potato Salad

Season Spring
Prep Time 15 minutes
Cook Time 8 to 10 minutes
Chill Time 30 minutes
Serves 2 to 3

Potato salad was brought to Japan during the Meiji era, more than a century ago. It is inspired by Russian salads made with potatoes, meat, hard-boiled eggs, mayonnaise, peas, and pickles. The Japanese version is less tart and generally made with ham and hard-boiled eggs (which I have omitted), mashed potatoes, cucumber, tomato, corn, and Japanese mayonnaise, making it richer and sweeter than Western versions.

1. Add the chopped potatoes to a pot filled with cold water and bring to a boil over high heat. Boil for 8 to 10 minutes, until the potatoes can be easily pierced with a fork, then drain. Use a potato masher or whisk to mash the potatoes. Let cool.

2. Put the cucumber slices in a colander set over a bowl and sprinkle with the coarse salt. Set aside to drain for at least 20 minutes.

3. When the cucumbers have drained, squeeze them firmly by hand to release as much excess water as possible, then add to the potatoes and stir to combine. Add the corn and tomatoes, mix it all together, and chill the mixture for at least 30 minutes. Add the mayonnaise and fine salt, stir to combine, and adjust the amount of salt as needed before serving.

2 large potatoes,
peeled and chopped

1 small cucumber,
cut into quarters
lengthwise, seeds
removed, and sliced

¾ teaspoon coarse salt

1 small tomato (80 g),
seeded and cubed

¼ cup (40 g) canned
corn

¼ cup (60 ml)
Japanese Mayonnaise
(page 29)

1 teaspoon fine salt

Eggplant Dengaku

Season Summer
Prep Time 10 minutes
Cook Time 15 to 20 minutes
Serves 2

Eggplant is one of the most popular vegetables in Japan, and one of the most classic ways to prepare it is dengaku, or brushed with a miso glaze. Dengaku can be made with tofu or with any type of vegetable, but I find that eggplant, with its sweet and mild flesh, pairs particularly well with miso's hit of umami. I like to top my version with cashews for a bit of crunch.

1. Roast the cashews in the oven at 350°F (180°C) for 5 to 10 minutes, until they begin to turn golden brown. Remove from the oven and let cool, then chop roughly and set aside.

2. While the cashews roast, cut the eggplants in half lengthwise and score the cut sides in a crosshatch pattern.

3. Heat a large skillet over medium heat. Add 1 tablespoon of the oil and, once hot, arrange the eggplant in the pan scored sides down, then cover and cook for 2 minutes.

4. Add 2 tablespoons of water, then re-cover the skillet. Cook for about 5 minutes longer, until the skin is tender.

5. Increase the oven temperature to 400°F (200°C).

6. Transfer the eggplant to a baking sheet, brush with the remaining oil, and roast cut-side up for 10 minutes, until the flesh is tender and soft and the skin is wrinkled. Monitor the eggplant while it cooks to avoid burning the skin.

7. Once cooked, arrange the eggplant halves on plates and pour over the miso glaze. Sprinkle with the sesame seeds, sliced scallions, and chopped cashews, and serve.

NOTE: Use Japanese eggplant in this recipe if you can find it, but if not, any kind of eggplant will work.

3 tablespoons cashews

2 eggplants (see Note)

⅓ cup (80 ml) canola oil

¼ cup (60 ml) Miso Glaze (page 20)

2 teaspoons white sesame seeds

1 scallion, thinly sliced on the bias

Green Bean Shiraae

Season *Summer*
Prep Time *10 minutes*
Rest Time *30 minutes*
Chill Time *30 minutes*
Cook Time *3 to 5 minutes*
Serves *2*

Shiraae is a vegetable salad made with tofu, white sesame seeds, and miso. The sesame seeds are ground into a paste then mixed into silken tofu to make a creamy sauce. It is a common dish in shōjin ryōri cuisine, the vegan cuisine of Buddhist monks. Shiraae is rich in protein, fiber, and nutrients; it satisfies both the body and spirit!

1. Wrap the tofu in paper towels and place on a plate. Place a heavy object (about 2 pounds) on top of the tofu to drain it. Let stand for at least 30 minutes, until the surface is mostly dry to the touch.

2. Bring a medium pot of water to a boil over high heat. Add the green beans and cook for 3 to 5 minutes, then drain immediately and rinse with cold water to stop the cooking and retain a slight crunch. Let dry.

3. Combine the sesame paste, mirin, soy sauce, and miso in a medium bowl and stir until smooth. Mix in the tofu, breaking it up as you stir. Be sure to leave some tofu pieces in the mixture; the texture should not be completely smooth.

4. Cut the green beans into bite-size pieces. Add to the tofu mixture with the salt and stir to combine.

5. Cover and let chill in the refrigerator for 30 minutes.

6. To serve, divide between two shallow bowls and sprinkle with the sesame seeds.

NOTE: Firm silken tofu is not the same thing as soft silken tofu; it's denser and better at holding its shape. My favorite brand is Morinaga. If you can't find firm silken tofu, you can substitute soft silken tofu and skip the pressing step. Just don't try to substitute firm block tofu.

- 5 ounces (140 g; about ½ cup plus 2 teaspoons) firm silken tofu (see Note)
- 1 cup (100 g) fresh green beans, trimmed
- 1 tablespoon white sesame paste or tahini
- 1 tablespoon mirin
- 1 teaspoon soy sauce
- ½ teaspoon white miso
- 1 pinch salt
- 2 teaspoons white sesame seeds

Cucumber Tsukemono

Season Summer
Prep Time 10 minutes
Rest Time 10 minutes
Chill Time 3 hours
Serves 3 to 4

Tsukemono are pickled vegetables. There are many varieties of tsukemono, and each uses a different ingredient such as salt, vinegar, miso, sake lees (a byproduct of sake fermentation), or sake to pickle the vegetables. The process normally takes a long time, but you can make a quick version, like this one, by drawing out the vegetables' excess moisture with salt then marinating them for a few hours in a vinaigrette.

1. Transfer the cucumber pieces to a colander set over a bowl, add the salt, and stir to coat. Let stand for 10 minutes to drain, then rinse well with water to remove the excess salt. Squeeze the cucumber pieces between your palms to remove as much water as possible, then set aside.

2. Add the ginger, soy sauce, rice vinegar, brown sugar, sake, sesame oil, and sansho to a small bowl and stir to combine.

3. Transfer the cucumber pieces and the ginger mixture into a large ziplock bag. Seal the bag, taking care to squeeze out as much air as possible, and let the cucumbers marinate for 3 hours in the refrigerator.

4. The tsukemono can be stored in the refrigerator for up to 3 days, but I recommend consuming within 1 day because the cucumbers lose their crunch quickly.

NOTE: Sansho can be found at Asian markets.

1 large cucumber or 2 small cucumbers, cut into quarters lengthwise, seeds removed, and chopped into bite-size pieces

2 teaspoons salt

One 1½-inch (4 cm) piece ginger, thinly sliced

¼ cup plus 3 tablespoons (100 ml) soy sauce

¼ cup plus 3 tablespoons (100 ml) rice vinegar

¼ cup (55 g) brown sugar

2 tablespoons sake

2 tablespoons toasted sesame oil

¼ teaspoon sansho (ground Japanese peppercorns; see Note)

Kabocha Soup

Season Fall
Prep Time 10 minutes
Cook Time 30 minutes
Serves 4

When fall is in full swing and winter's first winds begin to blow, is there anything better than warming up with a delicious soup? This comforting soup made with kabocha, a Japanese pumpkin with sweet hazelnut notes, is just the dish for enjoying the last produce of the season.

1. Preheat the oven to 400°F (200°C). Wrap the squash and garlic in aluminum foil and roast for 30 minutes, until both are tender.

2. Add the oil and onion to a pot over medium heat and sauté until the onion is caramelized, about 20 minutes.

3. Add ¼ cup plus 3 tablespoons (100 ml) water and the bouillon cube to a small bowl and stir to dissolve, then pour the broth into the pot with the onion. Add the milk.

4. Add the squash and garlic to the pot and puree the mixture with an immersion blender until mostly smooth.

5. Simmer over low heat until warmed through and season with salt and pepper before serving.

NOTE: You can find kabocha squash at Asian markets and some organic markets.

I prefer to use Oatly oat milk here because it has more fat than other plant-based milks and gives the soup a richer and creamier consistency.

1½ pounds (650 g) kabocha squash, peeled and chopped (see Notes)

2 garlic cloves, peeled

1 tablespoon canola oil

1 small onion, thinly sliced

½ vegetable bouillon cube

1½ cups (360 ml) oat or soy milk (see Notes)

SOY MILK

Kinpira Gobo

Season Fall
Prep Time 15 minutes
Rest Time 10 minutes
Cook Time 10 minutes
Serves 2

Gobo is very popular in Japan. It is the root of the burdock plant, which is known to be full of skin-healing nutrients as well as antioxidants and anti-inflammatory compounds. *Kinpira* refers to a method of preparation in which the ingredients are sautéed and then glazed with soy sauce and sugar. Kinpira gobo is great both warm and cold; it's often eaten as a salad or as a sautéed side dish with a portion of protein.

1. Peel the gobo using the back of a butter knife or the edge of a spoon to scrape away the skin.

2. Cut the gobo on the bias into ⅛-inch (3 mm) thick slices, then cut those slices into matchsticks.

3. Transfer the gobo to a large bowl of water and let stand for about 10 minutes to remove its bitterness. Drain the gobo in a colander and rinse until the water runs clear.

4. Add the sesame oil, the carrot, and the gobo to a large skillet over medium heat and sauté, stirring occasionally, until the vegetables become tender, 5 to 7 minutes.

5. Add the sake and stir. Sauté for 1 minute to cook off the alcohol.

6. Add the soy sauce to taste, the mirin, sugar, salt, and rayu oil, and stir until the liquid has reduced, 30 seconds to 1 minute. Season with salt.

7. Turn off the heat and allow the mixture to cool for a few minutes. Transfer to a bowl and sprinkle with the sesame seeds.

8. Serve immediately, or store in an airtight container in the refrigerator for up to 4 days.

1 whole gobo (7 oz/200 g), fresh or frozen

½ carrot (50 g), peeled and julienned

2 tablespoons toasted sesame oil

2 tablespoons sake

2 to 3 tablespoons soy sauce

2 tablespoons mirin

1 tablespoon sugar

2 pinches salt

1 teaspoon rayu chile oil

2 teaspoons white sesame seeds, toasted

Senmaizuke

Season *Fall*
Prep Time *10 minutes*
Rest Time *10 minutes*
Cook Time *5 minutes*
Chill Time *12 hours*
Serves *4 to 5*

Senmaizuke is a tart and irresistibly crunchy side dish I've loved since I was little. The word literally means "thousand-sliced pickles." It is a type of tsukemono—specifically, pickled turnips. This specialty from Kyoto adds a bright note when served alongside main dishes in a traditional meal. It also helps to cleanse the palate when eaten between two courses. Here I replace the turnip with daikon, just like the version my mother made. Using a mandoline makes it easy to thinly slice the daikon.

1. Add the daikon slices to a large bowl of cold water and let them stand for about 10 minutes, then drain. (This helps to remove the daikon's bitterness.)

2. Add the rice vinegar, sugar, and salt to a saucepan and bring to a boil over high heat. Turn off the heat and let cool. Add the kombu and chile pepper.

3. Pour the mixture over the daikon slices, then cover the bowl with plastic wrap and chill in the refrigerator for 12 hours.

4. Remove the kombu before serving. The senmaizuke can be stored in its marinade in an airtight container in the refrigerator for up to 4 days.

1 large daikon, peeled and thinly sliced

¾ cup plus 1 tablespoon (200 ml) rice vinegar

¼ cup (50 g) sugar

1 tablespoon salt

One 4-inch (10 cm) square kombu sheet

1 dried chile pepper, thinly sliced

Yaki Onigiri

Season Winter
Prep Time 20 minutes
Cook Time 20 minutes
Rest Time 15 minutes
Makes 2 to 3 onigiri

If you have already had the opportunity to visit Japan, you will have certainly tasted onigiri. Onigiri are rice balls that are sold in the 24-7 Japanese convenience stores known as konbinis. They are very popular in Japan because they're nutritious, satisfying, and quick and easy to eat on the go. Less well-known than the classic nori-wrapped onigiri, yaki onigiri are browned and then coated in a sweet and salty soy-sauce glaze. Yaki onigiri are traditionally grilled over binchotan charcoal, which adds a slightly smoky flavor. In this version they have the best of both worlds: They are cooked in a skillet for ease, yet there is still that robust smoky flavor from liquid smoke.

1. To cook the rice, follow the recipe on page 7. Once the rice has finished cooking, let it stand for 15 minutes (leave the lid on the pot or the rice cooker), then remove the lid and let the rice cool completely.

2. Add the mirin, sugar, and sake to a saucepan and bring to a boil over high heat. Add the soy sauce, reduce the heat, and allow the mixture to simmer for 10 minutes. Remove from the heat and add the liquid smoke to taste. Let cool until the sauce thickens slightly, 4 to 5 minutes.

3. Add the salt to the rice and mix to combine. Wet your hands with water or the rice vinegar (or wear latex gloves if you prefer) and roll the rice into 2 or 3 balls, then press to flatten and shape into rough triangles.

4. Arrange the onigiri in a hot nonstick skillet and brown on both sides, 3 to 5 minutes.

5. Reduce the heat to very low and brush the onigiri with the sauce. Continue to cook for a few seconds to caramelize the sauce, being careful not to let it burn, then serve.

NOTE: You can find liquid smoke at most supermarkets or online.

¾ cup (150 g) Japanese rice

¼ cup plus 2 tablespoons (90 ml) mirin

¼ cup plus 2 teaspoons (65 g) sugar

1 tablespoon plus 2 teaspoons sake

¼ cup plus 2 tablespoons (90 ml) soy sauce

2 to 3 drops liquid smoke (see Note)

¾ teaspoon salt

Rice wine vinegar

Kushiage

Season Winter
Prep Time 20 minutes
Cook Time 15 minutes
Rest Time 10 minutes
Serves 2

I discovered kushiage (also known as *kushikatsu*) during a holiday in Osaka just before I opened my restaurant, when I walked into a small shop hidden in a dark alley of Shinsekai, Osaka's working-class neighborhood famous for its cuisine. Kushiage is a very social dish in Osaka that is generally consumed among friends and alongside alcohol. It consists of skewers of meat, fish, or vegetables that are breaded with panko and deep fried, then dipped in a special ketchup-based sauce. The sauce is served in a large communal bowl, so it's considered bad manners to dip your skewer a second time after taking a bite.

1. Combine the eggplant, zucchini, and leeks in a large bowl, add the salt, and let stand for 10 minutes. Rinse with water to remove the excess salt and then blot gently with a towel to dry.

2. Cut the onion in half, then cut it lengthwise into 4 or 5 thick slices.

3. Thread the eggplant, zucchini, leeks, onion, asparagus, and renkon onto bamboo skewers; each skewer should have only one type of vegetable.

4. **To make the batter,** combine the flour and ¾ cup (180 ml) water in a bowl and whisk until no clumps remain. The texture should be thick but pourable.

5. Pour the panko into a blender and pulse until you have fine crumbs.

6. **To make the sauce,** combine the ketchup, Worcestershire sauce, soy sauce, and rice vinegar with 3 tablespoons water in a small bowl and set aside.

7. Add just enough of the oil to a large pan to cover the bottom by about 1 inch (2.5 cm). While it is warming over medium-high heat, prepare your work area: Arrange the bowls of batter and panko and your skewered vegetables near the pan. Line a cooling rack or large plate with paper towels.

8. Once the oil is between 340 and 350°F (170–180°C), dip a skewer of vegetables first in the batter, then in the panko, and then place it gently in the oil. (If you don't have a thermometer, you can test the oil by adding a small piece of panko; if it floats immediately, the oil is ready.) Repeat for each skewer, being careful not to overcrowd the pot. Cook in batches as necessary. Carefully remove the skewers once the panko coating has turned golden brown and the vegetables are tender, about 5 minutes per batch. Place the skewers on the prepared rack. (Remove the crumbs from the oil with a fine-mesh strainer in between batches to prevent the oil from taking on an unpleasant flavor.)

9. Enjoy by dipping each skewer entirely in the sauce.

NOTE: Use Japanese eggplant here if you can find it, but if you can't, any kind of eggplant will work.

½ **eggplant, chopped into bite-size pieces (see Note)**

½ **zucchini, cut into ½-inch (1.25 cm) thick slices**

2 **small, thin leeks, chopped into bite-size pieces**

1 **teaspoon salt**

1 **onion**

6 **asparagus spears, bottom halves peeled, cut into thirds**

6 **thick slices renkon (lotus root)**

BATTER

1 **cup (120 g) flour**

5 **cups (300 g) panko**

SAUCE

½ **cup (120 g) ketchup**

⅓ **cup (80 ml) vegan Worcestershire sauce**

2 **tablespoons usukuchi soy sauce**

1½ **teaspoons rice vinegar**

3 **to 4 cups (750–950 ml) sunflower or canola oil**

Korokke

Season Winter
Prep Time 1 hour
Cook Time 30 minutes
Makes 5 to 6 korokke

Korokke is a yōshoku dish that was brought from Portugal after Japan's opening to the West in the mid-1800s. Inspired by cheese croquettes, it instead calls for a potato-based filling because dairy products were not frequently consumed in Japan at the time. Today, there are many different versions, such as kabocha (page 65), sweet potato, meat, and okara (soy), to name a few.

1. Add the potatoes to a large pot of cold water and bring to a boil over high heat. Boil for 10 minutes, until the potatoes can be easily pierced with a fork, then drain. Mash the potatoes into a slightly chunky puree and season with salt. Set aside.

2. Add the oil and onion to a skillet and sauté over medium heat until the onions are caramelized, about 20 minutes. Add the tofu and corn and sauté for a few minutes longer, until golden. Turn off the heat and add the soy sauce.

3. Add the onion mixture to the potato along with 2 tablespoons of potato starch and stir to combine, then use your hands to form the mixture into 5 to 6 balls.

4. In one small bowl, combine the remaining potato starch with 3 tablespoons of flour and set aside. In a second small bowl, combine the remaining flour with ¼ cup plus 1 tablespoon (75 ml) water and stir until smooth, then set aside. Add the panko to a third small bowl.

5. Roll each potato ball first in the potato starch–flour mixture, then the flour-water mixture, and finally the panko. Use one hand for the "dry" bowls and the other for the "wet" to keep your hands cleaner.

6. Heat the sunflower oil in a pot over medium-high heat. Once the oil is between 340 and 350°F (170–180°C), gently lower the korokke into the oil using a slotted spoon; they must be completely immersed in the oil. (If you don't have a thermometer, you can test the oil by adding a small piece of panko; if it floats immediately, the oil is ready.) Fry until golden brown, 3 to 4 minutes, then carefully remove them from the oil and transfer to a sieve to drain. Serve with tonkatsu sauce.

- 3 russet potatoes (10.5 oz/300 g), peeled and chopped
- 1 onion, finely chopped
- 1 tablespoon canola oil
- 3 ounces (80 g; about ⅓ cup) smoked firm tofu, crumbled
- 3 tablespoons canned corn
- 1 tablespoon soy sauce
- ⅓ cup plus 1 tablespoon (50 g) potato starch or cornstarch
- ½ cup plus 2 tablespoons (75 g) flour
- ¾ cup (45 g) panko
- 2¼ cups (540 ml) sunflower or canola oil for frying
- Tonkatsu sauce, for serving

Yakisoba

Season Spring
Prep Time 20 minutes
Cook Time 5 minutes
Serves 2

Yakisoba is one of the most popular street food dishes in Japan because it is inexpensive and filling, not to mention irresistible thanks to its different textures and special sweet and savory sauce. Originally from China, this dish of sautéed noodles topped with vegetables and grilled meat became a favorite in Japan in the 1950s. Contrary to what the name suggests, the noodles are not made of soba (buckwheat) but wheat flour, like ramen noodles.

1. Heat the oil to a skillet or wok over medium-high heat. Add the onion, carrot, and salt, and sauté for 2 minutes, then add the cabbage and continue to sauté just until the cabbage softens, 3 to 4 minutes.

2. Add the noodles to a colander and rinse with hot water. Gently separate them by hand, then add them to the skillet and stir to combine. Reduce the heat and pour in your desired amount of yakisoba sauce. Stir well.

3. Divide the noodles between 2 plates. Garnish them with the chopped scallions, aonori, and beni shoga, and serve.

NOTE: I love the taste of Otafuku yakisoba sauce; it's used everywhere in Japan and is vegan! You can find yakisoba sauce, aonori, and beni shoga at Asian markets.

2 tablespoons
canola oil

½ onion, thinly sliced

½ carrot, cut into
matchsticks

1 pinch salt

3 green cabbage
leaves, chopped into
bite-size pieces

4 ounces (115 g)
cooked yakisoba
noodles

3 to 4 tablespoons
yakisoba sauce
(see Note)

GARNISH

2 chopped scallions

2 large pinches aonori
(flaked seaweed)

2 teaspoons beni shoga
(pickled ginger)

Osaka-Style Okonomiyaki

Season Spring
Prep Time 20 minutes
Cook Time 10 to 13 minutes
Rest Time 1 hour
Serves 2

Okonomiyaki is the ultimate street food of Japan's Kansai region. There are many styles of okonomiyaki (*okonomi* means "what you like" and *yaki* means "grilled"), but the most popular are from Osaka and Hiroshima. This recipe is based on the Osaka-style version, which is a thick pancake topped generously with cabbage and then cooked on a teppanyaki grill. However, for ease, I use a skillet instead of a grill here. Okonomiyaki can be served on its own, but if you like, you can serve it with a side of rice and enjoy it like a real Osakan!

1. Sift the flour, tapioca starch, and baking powder into a large bowl and mix. In another bowl, combine the silken tofu, kombu dashi powder, and ¾ cup plus 1 tablespoon (200 ml) water. Gradually add the wet mixture to the dry and whisk to combine, then stir in the cabbage, beni shoga, and mayonnaise. Let the mixture rest for 1 hour at room temperature. (You can skip this resting time if you are in a hurry.)

2. Heat 1 tablespoon of the oil in a nonstick skillet over high heat. Reduce the heat to medium and place 3 to 4 slices of tofu or 2 to 3 slices of vegan bacon (depending on how hungry you are) in the pan. Top with a ladleful of the batter and cover the skillet with a lid.

3. Check the okonomiyaki after about 5 minutes; if bubbles have begun to appear on the surface, flip it and cook the other side for about another 5 minutes. Otherwise, cook it for up to 3 minutes longer, checking regularly for bubbles, before flipping.

4. Transfer the okonomiyaki to a plate and repeat the cooking process with the remaining oil, tofu, and batter.

5. Cut each okonomiyaki into 6 equal pieces. Brush the pieces with the okonomiyaki sauce and top with the mayonnaise, aonori, and the remaining beni shoga. Serve immediately.

NOTE: My favorite okonomiyaki sauce is made by Otafuku. You can find okonomiyaki sauce, aonori, and beni shoga at Asian markets.

- 1¼ cups (150 g) flour
- 2 tablespoons plus 2 teaspoons tapioca starch
- 1 teaspoon baking powder
- 7 ounces (200 g; about ¾ cup) silken tofu
- 1 tablespoon kombu dashi powder
- 1¾ cups (120 g) shredded green cabbage
- ¼ cup (60 g) beni shoga (pickled ginger), plus 2 pinches for serving
- 2 tablespoons plus 2 teaspoons Japanese Mayonnaise (page 29), plus extra for serving
- 2 tablespoons canola oil
- 1 ounce (30 g; about 2 tablespoons) smoked firm tofu, thinly sliced, or vegan bacon
- Okonomiyaki sauce (see Note)
- 2 large pinches aonori (flaked seaweed)

Hiroshima–Style Okonomiyaki

Season Spring
Prep Time 20 minutes
Cook Time 10 minutes
Serves 2

Hiroshima-style okonomiyaki consist of thinner, lighter pancakes than the version from Osaka, and are served atop a bed of noodles. In keeping with the name *okonomi* ("what you like"), feel free to garnish with your choice of toppings.

1. Whisk together ¼ cup plus 3 tablespoons (105 ml) water with the flour, kombu dashi powder, and mayonnaise in a medium bowl.

2. Heat a nonstick skillet over medium heat. Pour in a ladleful of the batter to make a very thin pancake that measures about 8 inches (20 cm) in diameter. Add a large handful of the cabbage, chopped scallion, and bean sprouts. Top the vegetables with another small ladleful of the batter and cook for 2 to 3 minutes, then carefully use two spatulas to flip the okonomiyaki and cook for 2 to 3 minutes.

3. Transfer the cooked okonomiyaki to a plate and repeat the cooking process with the rest of the batter, cabbage, chopped scallion, and bean sprouts.

4. Divide the noodles between 2 plates and place the okonomiyaki on top.

5. Top with okonomiyaki sauce, mayonnaise, aonori, and beni shoga, and serve immediately.

NOTE: My favorite okonomiyaki sauce is made by Otafuku. You can find okonomiyaki sauce, aonori, and beni shoga at Asian markets.

½ cup (65 g) flour

2 teaspoons kombu dashi powder

1 teaspoon Japanese Mayonnaise (page 29), plus extra for serving

1⅓ cup plus 2 tablespoons (100 g) shredded green cabbage

1 scallion, chopped

½ cup (50 g) bean sprouts

4.25 ounces (120 g) cooked yakisoba noodles

GARNISH

Okonomiyaki sauce (see Note)

2 large pinches aonori (flaked seaweed)

Beni shoga (pickled ginger)

Tamago Sando

Season *Spring*
Prep Time *15 minutes*
Cook Time *5 minutes*
Serves *2*

Tamago sando (tamago for "egg" and sando for "sandwich") is the Japanese version of an egg salad sandwich. Its particularity lies in the characteristic taste of the sweet Japanese mayonnaise and especially the softness of the thick Japanese sandwich bread. In this vegan version, I replace the hard-boiled eggs with tofu and use kala namak to mimic the eggy flavor. For the best texture, be sure to let the tofu mixture cool completely before adding the mayonnaise.

1. Mash the soft tofu and 3 tablespoons (50 g) of the silken tofu in a bowl by hand until no large chunks remain. Add the turmeric for color and stir to combine.

2. Add the mixture to a skillet over medium heat and cook until heated through, 2 to 3 minutes, then return the mixture to the bowl and let it cool completely. (This step is optional, but I recommend doing it because the heat brings out the color of the turmeric.)

3. Add the mayonnaise, nutritional yeast, kala namak, mustard, soy sauce, onion, and salt to the tofu mixture and stir to combine. Adjust the amount of kala namak to taste.

4. Crumble the remaining silken tofu and add it to the bowl. Stir to combine, making sure to leave some chunks of tofu, which will mimic the egg white in a classic tamago sando.

5. Divide the tofu mixture between two slices of bread, top with the remaining bread slices, and serve.

NOTE: Soft block tofu is much softer than firm tofu but less delicate than silken tofu. You can find it at Asian markets.

- 7 ounces (200 g; about ¾ cup) soft block tofu (see Note)
- 9 ounces (250 g) silken tofu
- 3 to 4 pinches turmeric
- ¼ cup plus 3 tablespoons (100 g) Japanese Mayonnaise (page 29)
- 1½ teaspoons nutritional yeast
- ¾ teaspoon kala namak
- ½ teaspoon mustard
- ¼ teaspoon soy sauce
- ¼ small onion, diced
- 2 pinches salt
- 4 slices thick sandwich bread

Yaki Tomorokoshi

Season *Summer*
Prep Time *15 minutes*
Cook Time *15 minutes*
Serves *2*

At matsuri, or Japanese festivals, you will always find street food stalls selling grilled meat skewers, squid, or my favorite, yaki tomorokoshi, a whole ear of corn that is grilled with butter and soy sauce. It's a delicious mix of sweet, savory, and buttery, with an irresistible smoky flavor. Rather than grilling, here I cook the tomorokoshi in a skillet, adding a dash of liquid smoke to give it a hint of smoky grilled flavor. If you have a blowtorch, you can use it for extra charring. You can either serve the ears of corn whole or cut them into thirds to make them easier to eat.

1. Bring a pot of water to a boil over high heat, add the corn, and boil for about 10 minutes, then drain.

2. Melt the butter in a skillet over medium heat. Add the corn and sauté until the kernels begin to turn golden brown, about 5 minutes. Add the liquid smoke.

3. Turn off the heat and brush the corn with soy sauce to taste and the butter left in the skillet.

4. Serve immediately.

NOTE: You can find liquid smoke at most supermarkets or online.

2 whole ears of corn, shucked

1 tablespoon plus 2 teaspoons vegan butter

5 drops of liquid smoke (see Note)

1 to 2 tablespoons soy sauce

Gyoza

Season *Summer*
Prep Time *1 hour*
Rest Time *30 minutes*
Cook Time *10 minutes*
Makes *about 20 gyoza*

For me, gyoza evoke the summer holidays, when my sister and I had all the time in the world to help our mother cook. We worked together to make the gyoza by hand: One person prepared the dough and stuffing, one filled the wrappers, and one folded the dumplings. Time seemed to stand still while we made gyoza together and talked about the simple things in life. Like all types of dumplings, gyoza take a long time to prepare, so it's best to be accompanied by friends or family! Serve the gyoza with soy sauce and rice.

1. **To make the dough,** combine the hot water and salt in a small bowl and stir until the salt is dissolved. Add the flour to a separate bowl, then gradually pour the salt water into the flour, stirring continuously. Add up to 1 tablespoon more hot water if needed to bring the dough together into a ball.

2. Transfer the dough to a clean counter and knead for 10 minutes, then form it into a ball and wrap it with a clean towel. Let the dough stand for 30 minutes at room temperature.

3. Sprinkle the counter lightly with the potato starch and use a rolling pin to roll the dough into a disk about $\frac{1}{16}$-inch (2 mm) thick, or about the height of a penny.

4. Use a cookie cutter to cut disks about 3 inches (8 cm) wide. Lightly flour them to prevent sticking and then stack them on a plate. Cover with plastic wrap and place in the refrigerator until you're ready to form the dumplings.

5. **To make the filling,** add the cabbage, scallions, chives, mushrooms, garlic, ginger, ground meat, TVP, kombu dashi powder, sake, 1 teaspoon of the sesame oil, the soy sauce, and salt to a large bowl and mix together by hand.

6. Place 1 teaspoon of the filling in the center of each disk of dough. Dip your finger in a small bowl of water and use it to moisten the disk's circumference, then fold the dough in half, without sealing the dumpling.

7. Keeping the gyoza parallel to your body, using your thumbs, make diagonal pleats along the half edge closest to you, pressing on the folds to gradually seal the gyoza to the opposite edge.

8. After all the gyoza are sealed, heat about 2 teaspoons sesame oil in a nonstick skillet over medium heat. Arrange the gyoza in a single layer in the skillet and sauté without moving them for 2 to 3 minutes, until the gyoza are golden brown on the bottom.

9. Add about 3 tablespoons hot water to the skillet and cover immediately. Continue to cook until the water has evaporated, 1 to 2 minutes.

10. Remove the lid, add a small drizzle of sesame oil, and continue to cook the gyoza just until crispy, about 3 minutes. Serve hot.

DOUGH

¼ cup (60 ml) hot water (200°F/90°C), plus more for frying

½ teaspoon salt

1 cup (120 g) sifted flour

Potato starch

FILLING

Scant ½ cup (30 g) shredded green cabbage

¼ cup (25 g) thinly sliced scallions

3 tablespoons chopped chives

1 fresh shiitake mushroom, finely chopped

1 garlic clove, grated

One ¾-inch (2 cm) piece ginger, grated

1 cup (100 g) plant-based ground meat

¾ cup (70 g) textured vegetable protein (TVP), rehydrated and drained

1 teaspoon kombu dashi powder

1 teaspoon sake

1 teaspoon toasted sesame oil, plus more for frying

1 teaspoon soy sauce

1 pinch of salt

Ume-Mayo Onigiri

Season Summer
Prep Time 15 minutes
Cook Time 15 minutes
Makes 2 to 3 onigiri

There are several stories explaining why onigiri are triangular. One theory goes that it was once thought that the mountains were gods, and the Japanese shaped their rice dumplings like mountains to receive their protection. Triangle-shaped onigiri are most common, but onigiri come in other shapes as well: In the Kyushu region, they are round, while they are oval-shaped in the Tohoku and Chubu regions. Wherever they're from, they are the best grab-and-go snack, and these onigiri filled with mayonnaise and a sour-salty umeboshi plum are a favorite of mine.

1. To cook the rice, follow the recipe on page 7. Once the rice is cooked, let it cool, then season with salt.

2. Dampen your hands with rice vinegar to prevent sticking (or wear latex gloves), then divide the rice into 2 or 3 portions (to make 2 large or 3 smaller onigiri). Place 1 umeboshi in the center of each portion of rice along with 1 teaspoon mayonnaise. Gently roll the rice into balls completely encasing the umeboshi and mayonnaise, then press lightly to form a triangle.

3. Sprinkle the yukari shiso over the entire surface of the onigiri to taste.

4. Wrap half a nori sheet around each onigiri. Place a small piece of umeboshi on top of each before serving.

NOTE: Yukari is a spice blend made with dried red shiso leaves and salt. You can find it at Asian markets.

¾ cup (150 g) Japanese rice

Rice vinegar

3 to 4 umeboshi plums

3 teaspoons Japanese Mayonnaise (page 29)

Yukari (shiso rice seasoning; see Note)

1 to 1½ nori seaweed sheets

Kabocha Korokke

Season *Fall*
Prep time *45 minutes*
Cook Time *35 minutes*
Chill Time *15 minutes*
Makes *8 to 10 korokke*

I couldn't not share at least one street food recipe made with kabocha, the famous Japanese squash. Korokke are often sold individually at Japanese yatai (food carts) and enjoyed hot while walking down the street. On a chilly autumn day, there is nothing better than biting into a hot korokke, crispy on the outside yet soft and sweet on the inside. You can peel the kabocha squash if you want vibrant orange korokke, but it's completely fine to leave the skin on.

1. Add about 1 inch (2.5 cm) water to a large pot and bring to a boil over high heat. Carefully place a steaming basket inside, add the squash to the basket, and steam the squash for 20 minutes, until tender. Turn off the heat and transfer the squash to a large bowl. (Be careful not to cook it for too long, or it can absorb too much water.)

2. Add the soy sauce, butter, sugar, and salt to the bowl with the squash and mash until the mixture has a pureed consistency.

3. Once the puree has cooled enough to handle, use your hands to form 8 to 10 balls. Arrange on a large plate and cover with plastic wrap. Refrigerate for at least 15 minutes.

4. In one small bowl, combine the potato starch and 3 tablespoons of flour and set aside. In a second small bowl, combine the remaining flour and ¼ cup plus 1 tablespoon (75 ml) water and stir until smooth, then set aside. Add the panko to a third small bowl.

5. Roll each of the squash balls first in the potato starch–flour mixture, then the flour-water mixture, and finally the panko. Use one hand for the "dry" bowls and the other for the "wet" to keep your hands cleaner.

6. Heat the oil in a pot over medium heat. Once the oil is between 340 and 350°F (170–180°C), carefully lower 4 or 5 of the korokke into the oil using a slotted spoon; they must be completely immersed in the oil. (If you don't have a thermometer, you can test the oil by adding a small piece of panko; if it floats immediately, the oil is ready.) Fry until golden brown, about 8 minutes, then carefully remove the korokke from the oil and transfer to a sieve to drain. Repeat with the remaining korokke in as many batches as necessary. Serve immediately.

- 3 cups (400 g) chopped kabocha squash
- 1 tablespoon soy sauce
- 2 teaspoons vegan butter
- 1¼ teaspoons sugar
- ½ teaspoon salt
- 3 tablespoons potato starch or cornstarch
- ½ cup plus 2 tablespoons (75 g) flour
- ¾ cup (45 g) panko
- 2¼ cups (540 ml) sunflower or canola oil

Tempura

Season Fall
Prep Time 20 min
Cook Time 2 to 3 minutes
Serves 2

When we think of Japanese street food, it's usually fried foods like korokke, karaage, and kushiage that come to mind. And, of course, tempura! To be honest, I wasn't sure how to classify this dish because it is often served in a traditional meal at ryokans (traditional Japanese inns) as well as at yatai (food carts) and in Japanese diners. What's certain, however, is that it's incredibly easy to make tempura vegan: just fry your favorite vegetable! Tempura batter traditionally contains egg, but here I use silken tofu as a binder instead. Fall vegetables like renkon (lotus root), satsumaimo (sweet potato), kabocha, and mushrooms are perfect for this snack. There's no need to peel the vegetables (except the renkon), as the skin is delicious and softens as it cooks.

1. Combine the tofu and mayonnaise in a small bowl, then stir in 1¼ cups (300 ml) water.

2. Add the flour to a second bowl. Gradually pour the tofu mixture into the flour, stirring continuously until smooth. Store the batter in the refrigerator until you're ready to use it.

3. Set a large pot over medium heat and add just enough of the oil to cover the bottom by about 1 inch (2.5 cm).

4. Once the oil is between 340 and 350°F (170–180°C), dip the sliced vegetables in the chilled batter. (If you don't have a thermometer, you can test the oil by adding a small drop of batter; if it sizzles immediately, the oil is ready.) Let the excess batter drip off so the vegetables are only thinly coated. (If the batter has thickened too much in the refrigerator, dilute it with a little cold water.)

5. Fry the tempura in batches, 1 batch per vegetable, for at least 2 minutes or until the vegetable is tender enough to be pierced easily with a toothpick. Keep your eye on the temperature of the oil; 340°F is optimum for perfectly crispy tempura. Transfer the tempura to a paper towel–lined cooling rack to drain. Serve immediately.

NOTE: Satsumaimo is available at many Asian markets, but if you can't find it you can use an orange sweet potato. King trumpet mushrooms are also known as king oyster mushrooms.

3 tablespoons silken tofu

1 tablespoon Japanese Mayonnaise (page 29)

1½ cups (200 g) cake flour

1 small satsumaimo (Japanese sweet potato; see Note), thinly sliced

⅙ kabocha squash, thinly sliced

2½-inch (6 cm) piece renkon (lotus root), fresh or frozen, thinly sliced

3 king trumpet mushrooms, thinly sliced (see Note)

3 to 4 cups (750–950 ml) sunflower or canola oil

Zenzai

Season Winter
Prep Time 5 minutes
Cook Time 10 to 15 minutes
Serves 2

Zenzai is a traditional Japanese dessert made up of mochi (chewy rice cakes) and sweet red bean soup. Zenzai is said to ward off illness and evil spirits, which is why it is commonly placed on household altars as an offering. It is usually eaten during fall and winter, but a chilled version is enjoyed in the summer. These are made with tsubu-an (chunky red bean paste).

2 kirimochi
(see Note), or
2 Mitarashi Dango
(page 150)

2 tablespoons plus
2 teaspoons (50 g)
chunky Anko Paste
(page 30)

1 pinch salt

1. Preheat the oven to 350°F (180°C). Bake the kirimochi for at least 10 to 15 minutes, until they have puffed slightly and are lightly browned. If you are using Mitarashi Dango, follow the recipe on page 150.

2. While the kirimochi bakes, combine ¼ cup (60 ml) water with the anko paste and salt in a saucepan over medium heat, and cook until the consistency becomes soupy, about 5 minutes. Add up to 4 teaspoons more water to thin the soup as desired. Divide it between 2 small bowls, top with a kirimochi, and serve.

NOTE: You can find kirimochi, dried and cut mochi, at Asian markets. If you like, you can cut the mochi into halves or thirds before adding it to the bowls.

Daigaku Imo

Season Winter
Prep Time 20 minutes
Soak Time 15 minutes
Cook Time 20 minutes
Serves 2 to 3

The Japanese sweet potato, or satsumaimo, is a very sweet variety with yellow flesh and purple skin. It is delicious eaten plain or when combined with other sweet or savory ingredients. Daigaku imo is an incredibly popular Japanese snack made by caramelizing a satsumaimo in sugar and butter and then sprinkling with black sesame seeds for a bit of color and crunch. It's a real treat for anyone with a sweet tooth!

1. Soak the satsumaimo in a large bowl of water for about 15 minutes, then drain. (This softens it slightly, so it achieves the right texture after being cooked.)

2. Melt the butter in a skillet over medium heat. Add the satsumaimo and sauté until golden, about 4 minutes, then add the sugar, mirin, and soy sauce. Cover the skillet, reduce the heat to low, and simmer for 8 to 10 minutes, until the satsumaimo is tender, flipping the sweet potato pieces halfway through. If the sauce reduces before the sweet potato becomes tender, add a little water and re-cover.

3. Uncover the skillet and continue to cook until the sauce is thick and sticky, about 1 minute.

4. Remove the satsumaimo from the heat and sprinkle with the sesame seeds before serving.

- 1 satsumaimo (10 oz/280 g), cubed
- 2 tablespoons vegan butter
- 2 tablespoons sugar
- 1 tablespoon mirin
- 1½ teaspoons soy sauce
- 2 teaspoons black sesame seeds

Sanshoku Dango Mochi

Season Spring
Prep Time 45 minutes
Cook Time 5 minutes
Makes 9 skewers

The arrival of spring in Japan is marked by hanami, the traditional custom of viewing the cherry blossoms, when Japanese people gather to picnic under the blossoming trees. Sanshoku dango (literally "dango with three colors") is a dessert comprised of three colorful skewered rice dumplings—one pink to symbolize the cherry blossoms, one white to recall the past winter's snow, and one green to represent spring grass—and is commonly enjoyed at these picnics.

1. Combine the rice flour and sugar in a bowl, then divide the mixture evenly between three different bowls.

2. Fill three more small bowls with 3 tablespoons (45 ml) water each. Add the red food coloring to one bowl and mix. Add the matcha to the second bowl and mix. (The third bowl should contain only water.)

3. Pour the red water into one of the bowls of rice flour and stir to combine. Repeat with the other two bowls of water and rice flour. Add more water, ½ teaspoon at a time, if necessary; the dough should come together but not be sticky.

4. You will have one bowl each of pink, green, and white dough. Form 9 small balls of each color by rolling the dough between the hollows of your palms.

5. Fill a large bowl with ice and water and set aside. Bring a large pot of water to a boil over high heat, then add the white balls and boil until they float to the surface, 1 to 2 minutes.

6. Use a slotted spoon or spider skimmer to transfer the white dango to the ice bath.

7. Repeat this process for the pink dango and finally the green.

8. Remove the dango from the ice bath and thread one of each color onto a total of 9 skewers.

9. Serve the dango as is, or brush them with the anko paste, if using, for a richer treat.

- 1¼ cups (150 g) glutinous rice flour
- ¼ cup plus 2 tablespoons (75 g) sugar
- 2 drops vegan red food coloring
- ¼ teaspoon matcha powder
- Anko Paste (page 30), optional

GLUTINOUS RICE FLOUR

Sakura Mochi

Season Spring
Prep Time 30 minutes
Cook Time 5 to 15 minutes
Makes 6 mochi

Sakura mochi is a wagashi (a sweet treat usually enjoyed with green tea) that is traditionally eaten during Hinamatsuri, the Girls' Day festival. It is a pink mochi filled with anko (red bean) paste and wrapped in a salt-pickled sakura (cherry) leaf. There are two varieties of sakura mochi: In the Kanto region, a thin pancake made from glutinous rice flour is wrapped around a filling of anko paste. In the Kansai region, coarse glutinous rice flour, domyojiko, is made into a thick dough that is filled with the anko paste. This simpler version of sakura mochi is similar to a daifuku, a wagashi of chewy glutinous rice flour with a red bean filling, wrapped in a sakura leaf.

1. Divide the anko paste into 6 equal portions and place in the refrigerator.

2. Lightly sprinkle a clean work surface with potato starch.

3. Combine the glutinous rice flour and sugar in a bowl. Combine ½ cup plus 2 tablespoons (150 ml) water and your desired amount of red food coloring in a second bowl, then pour the red water into the rice flour mixture and stir until homogenous.

4. To cook the mochi, cover the bowl with plastic wrap and microwave it at 50 percent power for 3 minutes. Remove the bowl from the microwave, stir the mixture with a wet spatula (the mixture should be half liquid and half solid), then microwave at 50 percent power for 1½ to 2 more minutes, until fully solidified. Stir again with a spatula. Alternatively, bring a small pot of water to a boil over high heat, place the bowl of mochi over the pot, and heat for 15 minutes, stirring continuously with a spatula.

5. The mochi is cooked when it becomes slightly translucent.

6. Once the mochi is cooked, transfer to the countertop dusted with potato starch. Cut it into 6 equal parts and sprinkle with more potato starch, then roll into 6 balls. Flatten the balls to form 6 disks.

7. Dust your hands with potato starch and place 1 portion of the chilled anko paste in the middle of each mochi disk. Close the dough around the anko paste and firmly pinch the edges together to seal. Dust the counter with more starch, then gently roll the mochi into round balls. Wrap a sakura leaf around each mochi before serving.

½ cup plus 1 tablespoon (180 g) Anko Paste (page 30)

Potato starch

¾ cup plus 1 tablespoon (100 g) glutinous rice flour

1 tablespoon plus 2 teaspoons sugar

1 to 2 drops vegan red food coloring

6 pickled sakura leaves (see Note)

NOTE: You can find salt-pickled sakura leaves at some Asian markets or online.

GLUTINOUS RICE FLOUR

Melon Pan

Season Spring
Prep Time 1 hour
Rest Time 3 to 3½ hours
Cook Time 25 to 35 minutes
Makes 8 melon pan

Melon pan was my absolute favorite treat when I was a child. Its name comes from the sweet cookie crust surrounding the brioche center, which looks like the skin of a melon. Some pastry chefs even add actual melon to the batter to incorporate the taste of the fruit into the bread. I prefer plain melon pan, but you can add matcha, chocolate chips, or strawberries! For a richer treat, you can even fill them with vegan whipped cream.

1. **To make the cookie crust,** combine the cake flour, soy milk, canola oil, brown sugar, and vanilla extract in a large bowl. Form the dough into a ball, wrap in plastic wrap, and store in the refrigerator.

2. **To make the brioche,** let the butter and remaining soy milk come to room temperature. Stir the yeast into the lukewarm soy milk and let it sit for 10 minutes, until the liquid appears frothy on the surface.

3. Combine the flour, brown sugar, and salt in the bowl of a stand mixer. Add the milk mixture and mix on low speed for 10 minutes, until the dough is smooth and stretchy.

4. Cover the bowl and let the dough stand for 2 hours somewhere warm, ideally 85 to 95°F (30–35°C), until the dough doubles in volume.

5. Deflate the brioche and spread the dough onto a clean work surface. Fold the dough in half and then cut it into 8 equal parts. Roll each piece into a ball.

6. Remove the cookie dough from the refrigerator and form 8 balls. Flatten the cookie balls into thin disks, then wrap them around the brioche balls. Lightly score the surface of each melon pan in a crosshatch pattern.

7. Place the melon pan on a baking sheet, cover with a clean cloth, and let rise at room temperature until doubled in size, 1 to 1½ hours.

8. Preheat the oven to 350°F (175°C). Once the melon pan have risen, bake them for 25 to 30 minutes.

9. Let the melon pan cool slightly before serving.

COOKIE CRUST

- 1¼ cups (150 g) cake flour or all-purpose flour
- 3 tablespoons soy milk
- 2 tablespoons plus 1 teaspoon canola oil
- ¼ cup (55 g) brown sugar
- 1½ teaspoons vanilla extract

BRIOCHE

- ⅓ cup (70 g) vegan butter
- ½ cup (120 ml) soy milk
- 1¼ teaspoons dry yeast
- 2 cups plus 1 tablespoon (250 g) bread flour
- 3 tablespoons plus 1 teaspoon brown sugar
- ¼ teaspoon salt

Ichigo Daifuku

Season Spring
Prep Time 1 hour
Cook Time 5 to 15 minutes
Makes 6 daifuku

Daifuku is a type of mochi filled with sweet red bean paste. One of the most popular wagashi (Japanese treats usually enjoyed with green tea), it is found almost everywhere in Japan, even in konbinis (24-7 convenience stores). *Ichigo* means "strawberry," so as the name suggests, a strawberry is hidden inside. This wagashi is especially delicious because of how the tartness of the fruit complements the sweet anko paste.

1. Divide the anko paste into 6 equal portions, then wrap each strawberry completely in it. Arrange the anko-covered strawberries on a plate, cover with plastic wrap, and refrigerate.

2. Lightly sprinkle a clean work surface with potato starch.

3. Combine the glutinous rice flour and sugar in a bowl. Add ½ cup plus 2 tablespoons (150 ml) water and stir until homogenous.

4. To cook the mochi, cover the bowl with plastic wrap and microwave it at 50 percent power for 3 minutes. Remove the bowl from the microwave (the mixture should be half liquid and half solid), stir the mixture with a wet spatula, then microwave at 50 percent power for 1½ to 2 more minutes, until fully solidified. Stir again with a spatula. Alternatively, bring a small pot of water to a boil over high heat, place the bowl of mochi over the pot, and heat for 15 minutes, stirring continuously with a spatula.

5. The mochi is cooked when it becomes slightly translucent.

6. Once the mochi is cooked, transfer to the countertop dusted with potato starch. Cut it into 6 equal parts and sprinkle with more potato starch, then roll into 6 balls. Flatten the balls to form 6 disks.

7. Dust your hands with potato starch and place a chilled anko-coated strawberry in the center of each disk. Wrap the mochi dough around each strawberry, then firmly pinch the edges together to seal. Dust the counter with more starch, then gently roll the mochi into round balls.

8. Enjoy the mochi within 1 day.

½ cup plus
1 tablespoon
(180 g) Anko Paste
(page 30)

6 large strawberries

Potato starch

¾ cup plus
1 tablespoon (100 g)
glutinous rice flour

1 tablespoon plus
2 teaspoons sugar

Kinako Ice Cream

Season Summer
Prep Time 1¼ to 2¼ hours
Cook Time 30 minutes
Makes about 3½ pints (1 kg) ice cream

It's not summer without ice cream! Frozen desserts of every kind are enjoyed throughout Japan's hot summers. They come in all forms: on sticks, in pots, in the shape of fruit, as soda-flavored ice pops, and even shaved ice, the famous kakigōri. And of course, there's ice cream. The most common flavors are vanilla, matcha, and chocolate, but I love this version made with kinako, or roasted soybean powder, which tastes a bit like peanuts.

1. Add 1½ cups plus 1 tablespoon (385 ml) of the soy milk to a pot along with the cream, kinako, and granulated sugar. Warm over medium heat, stirring occasionally.

2. While the milk mixture heats, combine the cornstarch and the remaining milk in a small bowl, stirring until the starch has completely dissolved.

3. Add the cornstarch mixture to the pot and whisk to combine. Continue whisking until the kinako mixture thickens, 5 to 10 minutes, then remove it from the heat and let cool slightly. Cover with plastic wrap, pressing the plastic directly against the surface of the mixture, and place in the refrigerator to cool completely.

4. Once cold, transfer the kinako mixture to an ice cream maker and run the machine according to the manufacturer's instructions. (If you do not have an ice cream maker, place the mixture in the freezer and process it in a blender every 30 minutes until smooth.)

5. **To make the syrup,** add the kurozato and 1 tablespoon plus 2 teaspoons water to a saucepan over high heat. Bring to a boil and then reduce the heat to low. Cook for 45 seconds, stirring continuously, to reduce the syrup. It should be thick but pourable. Transfer the syrup to a heat-safe container and let cool completely.

6. **To serve,** scoop the ice cream into individual bowls and drizzle with the syrup. (Store any leftover ice cream in an airtight container in the freezer.)

NOTE: You can find kinako powder and kurozato at Asian markets or online.

2 cups plus 1 tablespoon (500 ml) soy milk

2 cups plus 1 tablespoon (500 ml) plant-based cream

¾ cup plus 1 tablespoon (100 g) kinako powder (see Note)

½ cup plus 2 tablespoons (125 g) granulated sugar

⅓ cup (40 g) cornstarch

2 tablespoons kurozato (unrefined Japanese sugar; see Note) or dark brown sugar

Black Sesame Ice Cream

Season *Summer*
Prep Time *1¼ to 2¼ hours*
Cook Time *30 minutes*
Makes *about 3½ pints (1 kg) ice cream*

Many Japanese people are lactose intolerant, so it is not uncommon to find soy-milk ice cream in Japan. The secret to making a creamy ice cream with plant milk is starch. Adding cornstarch thickens the plant milk and gives the ice cream luscious body. Here, black sesame paste adds a boldly nutty, earthy flavor to the ice cream.

1. Add 1½ cups plus 1 tablespoon (385 ml) of the milk to a saucepan along with the cream, sugar, and black sesame paste. Use an immersion blender to puree the mixture until smooth, then warm over medium heat, stirring occasionally.

2. While the milk mixture heats, combine the cornstarch and the remaining milk in a small bowl, stirring until the starch has completely dissolved.

3. Add the cornstarch mixture to the pot and whisk to combine. Continue whisking until the sesame mixture thickens, 5 to 10 minutes, then remove it from the heat and let cool slightly. Cover with plastic wrap, pressing the plastic directly against the surface of the mixture, and place in the refrigerator to cool completely.

4. Once cold, stir in the sesame seeds, then transfer the sesame mixture to an ice cream maker and run the machine according to the manufacturer's instructions. (If you do not have an ice cream maker, place the mixture in the freezer and process it in a blender every 30 minutes until smooth.)

5. To serve, scoop the ice cream into individual bowls. (Any leftover ice cream can be stored in an airtight container in the freezer.)

NOTE: You can find black sesame paste at Asian markets.

2 cups plus 1 tablespoon (500 ml) soy milk

2 cups plus 1 tablespoon (500 ml) plant-based cream

½ cup plus 2 tablespoons (125 g) sugar

2 tablespoons plus 2 teaspoons black sesame paste (see Note)

⅓ cup (40 g) cornstarch

1 tablespoon black sesame seeds

Mitarashi Dango

Season Summer
Prep Time 10 minutes
Cook Time 5 minutes
Makes about 10 dango

Like daifuku, dango are traditional mochi desserts made with glutinous rice flour mixed with water, however, they are less well-known. In this version, served with sweet-salty mitarashi sauce, they are chewy and smoky, especially if you roast them with a blowtorch. This recipe is very easy to make and pairs perfectly with a cup of green tea.

1. Combine ⅓ cup (80 ml) water with the flour in a bowl and mix until a dough forms. It should not be sticky. Form balls about 1 inch (2.5 cm) in diameter by first squishing and then rolling a portion of the dough between your palms. The dango will puff slightly during cooking.

2. Fill a large bowl with ice and water and set aside. Bring a large pot of water to a boil over high heat, then add the dango and boil until they float to the surface, 1 to 2 minutes. Continue to boil for another 1 to 2 minutes, depending on their size. Transfer the dango to the bowl of ice water using a slotted spoon or spider skimmer.

3. Once they have cooled, thread 3 to 4 dango onto each skewer and roast them with a blowtorch until lightly charred in places. (If you don't have a blowtorch, you can toast them in a nonstick pan over medium-high heat until browned.)

4. Pour the mitarashi sauce onto a plate and roll the skewers in the sauce to coat. Serve immediately.

¾ cup plus 1 tablespoon (100 g) glutinous rice flour

Mitarashi Sauce, for serving (page 16)

GLUTINOUS RICE FLOUR

Dorayaki

Season Fall
Prep Time 20 minutes
Rest Time 10 minutes
Cook Time 5 minutes
Makes 6 dorayaki

If you've seen Naomi Kawase's 2015 film *Sweet Bean*, you know what dorayaki look like. These anko-filled pancakes were one of my favorite after-school snacks. The cake traditionally contains egg whites, giving it a fluffy texture. Making this pancake vegan was a challenge, but with the right tools and ingredients, you can re-create these delicacies at home. If you have a gas burner, the pancakes will brown more evenly; if you have an electric burner, vary the temperature and test with a small amount of batter to find the correct heat level before cooking the dorayaki.

1. Combine the milk, oil, maple syrup, and vanilla in a bowl. In a second bowl, combine the flour, sugar, cornstarch, salt, and baking powder.

2. Sift the dry mixture over the liquid and whisk to combine. Let stand for about 10 minutes.

3. Heat a nonstick skillet over medium heat. Pour in a small ladleful of batter. After about 3 minutes, once bubbles appear on the surface, use a spatula to flip the dorayaki and cook for 1 minute longer, until the underside is golden. Repeat with the remaining batter. (You should have 12 pancakes in all.)

4. Transfer the pancakes to an airtight container and let stand for a few hours at room temperature. (This step is optional but will improve the texture of the pancakes.)

5. Sandwich 1 tablespoon of anko paste between two pancakes and press together lightly before serving.

½ cup plus
  2 tablespoons
  (150 ml) soy milk

2 tablespoons
  canola oil

1 tablespoon plus
  2 teaspoons maple
  syrup

1 tablespoon vanilla
  extract

1¼ cups (150 g)
  cake flour

⅓ cup (60 g) sugar

1 tablespoon
  cornstarch

1 teaspoon salt

½ teaspoon baking
  powder

6 tablespoons Anko
  Paste (page 30)

Yōkan

Season Fall
Prep Time 2½ hours
Cook Time 6 minutes
Rest Time 20 minutes
Chill Time 2 hours
Serves 10

Out of all the wagashi (traditional Japanese sweet treats), yōkan is my favorite. It is a sort of jelly made from sweet anko paste. There are two types of yokan: neri yōkan, which has a firmer texture, and mizu yōkan, which contains more water and breaks apart more easily and is what I use here. This recipe includes two jellies: one wine-red thanks to anko paste, the other transparent to lay on the surface.

1. **To make the anko jelly,** combine the cold water and kanten in a pot. Bring to a boil over high heat and cook, stirring continuously, for 2 minutes. Reduce the heat and add the anko paste. Stir well for 1 minute, then transfer the mixture to a rectangular mold, such as a loaf pan, that's large enough to hold at least 2½ cups (600 ml) and let cool at room temperature for about 10 minutes.

2. **To make the transparent jelly,** in another pot, combine the cold water with the agar powder. Bring to a boil over high heat and use a slotted spoon to remove any foam that forms on the surface. Reduce the heat and simmer for 2 minutes. Add the sugar and stir until it has completely dissolved. Continue skimming any foam. Simmer for 1 minute longer, then turn off the heat.

3. Pour the agar mixture over the entire surface of the anko yōkan in the mold. Pop the bubbles that form on the surface by pricking them with a toothpick.

4. Arrange the momiji, if using, on the surface. Let the yōkan cool for about 10 minutes, until it comes to room temperature, then cover and refrigerate for 2 to 4 hours before cutting into rectangular pieces. Serve chilled. Any leftovers can be wrapped in plastic wrap to keep them from drying out, placed in an airtight container, and stored in the refrigerator for up to 2 days.

ANKO JELLY

½ cup plus 1 teaspoon (125 ml) cold water

1 teaspoon kanten or ½ teaspoon agar powder (see Notes)

¾ cup plus 1 tablespoon (250 g) smooth Anko Paste (page 30)

TRANSPARENT JELLY

¾ cup plus 1 tablespoon (200 ml) cold water

½ teaspoon agar powder

½ cup (100 g) sugar

GARNISH

10 momiji (Japanese maple leaves; see Notes) or edible flowers, optional

NOTE: Kanten is similar to agar powder and is used as a thickener. I prefer to use kanten in this recipe when possible as it results in a smoother texture, but since it's only found in select Japanese markets, you can use agar powder if you can't find it.

You can find momiji at some Asian markets or online.

Acknowledgments

I dedicate this book to my mother, who has always been a source of inspiration for me.

I thank my father for having supported me in all my projects.

Thank you to Vlad, my biggest fan and the most extraordinary husband.

Many thanks to Marjorie, my editor, and to Marie, without whom this project would not have been possible.

A huge thank you to Sanae for her illustrations, which bring this book to life, and to Manon, for her magnificent photos.

I also want to thank the team of Mori Café—Mika, Melissa, and Emma—for their help and kindness every day.

Index

NOTE: Page references in *italics* refer to photographs.

About the Author

Julia Boucachard grew up splitting her time between Japan and France. After becoming vegetarian and then vegan, she found her options when dining out drastically limited, so she became a self-taught cook and started a catering business. She now runs Mori Café in Paris, where she shares plant-based recipes inspired by the food of her childhood.

moricafeparis.com/en |  moricafeparis